"By breaking down effective strategies into simple-to-digest, bite-size pieces, this is a book that will really help you take small steps toward a life that matters to you. The authors bring a wonderful combination of authenticity and expertise. It is clear they wouldn't ask you to do anything that they themselves are not willing to do, and it's great to know these ideas have a good scientific foundation behind them too."

—**Ben Sedley, PhD**, clinical psychologist, and
author of *Stuff That Sucks*

"If you're like me and your attention span is shrinking, this is the perfect book for you. 'Teeny Tiny Practices?' 'Microskills?' Yes, please! Using helpful examples and relatable personal experiences, the authors provide the scaffolding to understand the 'why' behind each bite-size acceptance and commitment therapy (ACT) practice. *Stop Avoiding Stuff* is easy to digest, practical, and really fun to read. If you want to live a mightier life, I highly recommend this book!"

—**Jill A. Stoddard, PhD**,
author of *Be Mighty*

T0003152

"*Stop Avoiding Stuff* is the perfect balance of skills, wisdom, authenticity, and humor. I fell in love with this book. I saw myself—all too well—in Jen, Lisa, and Matt's personal examples. As I read this book, I saw subtle ways and areas where I avoid stuff, and found compassionate microskills to help move me closer toward a life guided by values rather than dictated by old fears."

—**Aisling Leonard-Curtin, CPsychol, PsSI**, chartered psychologist with The Psychological Society of Ireland; peer-reviewed ACT trainer; and coauthor of the #1 best seller, *The Power of Small*

"Boone, Gregg, and Coyne have pulled off a marvelous feat— they have distilled down many of the core principles of ACT into a format that is fun to read! The book strikes just the right tone—you feel like you're learning and even being challenged, without being lectured to or judged. I love the opportunities for teeny tiny practice—just the right size to make realistic change!"

—**Sonja V. Batten, PhD**, psychologist, executive coach, past president and fellow of the Association for Contextual Behavioral Science (ACBS), author of *Essentials of Acceptance and Commitment Therapy*, and coauthor of *Committed Action in Practice*

"*Stop Avoiding Stuff* offers concrete, practical, doable microskills that will help you get out of the avoidance trap. Grounded in scientific research, this approachable yet thorough book breaks down the tools needed for sustained behavior change into manageable steps. I'd recommend this to anyone who is ready to take action in their life, and is looking for the tools to help them move toward what really matters to them."

> —**Jenna LeJeune, PhD**, licensed psychologist; president of Portland Psychotherapy Clinic, Research, and Training Center; and coauthor of *Values in Therapy*

"This delightful little book is chock-full of kitchen-table wisdom, presented in a simple, humble, genuine, and accessible way. It both humanizes our natural tendency to avoid stuff we don't like, while giving us a variety of healthy ways to turn back toward the stuff we are running from. This book is perfect for the time-challenged reader who might be willing to spend ten minutes each day building a conscious, intentional way of living. Beware though, this book can easily become a real 'page-turner,' as you get more and more intrigued about the impact of little behaviors on your ongoing sense of personal vitality and life meaning."

> —**Kirk Strosahl, PhD**, cofounder of ACT, and coauthor of *The Mindfulness and Acceptance Workbook for Depression*

"Everything in my life that works better now than it did before is a result of me stopping avoiding stuff. As this delightful book makes perfectly clear, *stuff* is not just activities that we avoid, but thoughts, feelings, and experiences in the body. *Stop Avoiding Stuff* does an impressive job highlighting all the ways we can learn to be more flexible, and how we can use that flexibility to suffer less and lean into more of what life has to offer. It was easy not to avoid writing this endorsement."

—**Jon Hershfield, MFT**, director of The OCD and Anxiety Center at Sheppard Pratt, author of *When a Family Member Has OCD* and *Overcoming Harm OCD*, and coauthor of *The Mindfulness Workbook for OCD* and *Everyday Mindfulness for OCD*

"Life doesn't come with a rule book, but if it did, this would be a pretty cool one. It's bite-size, fun to read, and covers the most important things. Once you are oriented, you can bounce around and acquire the skills that most interest you or that you really need right now. You could even put it in the bathroom and read it there. Not every book that can change your life needs to be a tome. Instead, stop avoiding stuff—one tiny bit at a time."

—**Steven C. Hayes, PhD**, Nevada Foundation Professor in the department of psychology at the University of Nevada, Reno; and originator and codeveloper of ACT

"Is fear holding you back in life at times? Then this book is for you. It's packed with practical and manageable suggestions on how to thrive and step out of stuff that sucks, and into stuff that matters. It takes you through an easy-to-read, at times personal, down-to-earth, humorous, and loving journey too. Read this book. Your life is waiting for you to join it."

> —**Rikke Kjelgaard, MSc**, author; licensed psychologist; chief rock and roller and expert in ACT; and creator of Fierce, Fabulous, and Female

"In a world of unknowns, there are plenty of reasons to bury our heads in the sand. What if, by doing teeny tiny exercises, we faced our stuff, talked about our stuff, and, in the process of making our stuff feel better, we improved everyone else's stuff as well. Now, that would be some *great* stuff, and you can learn how to get started on all that stuff right here in this book."

> —**Patrick B. McGrath, PhD**, licensed clinical psychologist, head of clinical services at NOCD, and president of Anxiety Centers of Illinois

"We all come by our avoidance naturally. But when it stops us from handling our daily tasks or moving toward our life's goals, it's time to be courageous. The good news is that facing life boldly isn't a personality trait; it's a set of skills, and *Stop Avoiding Stuff* delivers them in easily digestible bites. Fully engaging in our lives will always require moments of effort. That's exactly what you'll get in this go-to guide: small actions you can take, moment by moment, that add up to the big results you want."

—Reid Wilson, PhD, author of
Stopping the Noise in Your Head

STOP AVOIDING STUFF

25 Microskills to Face Your Fears & Do It Anyway

MATTHEW S. BOONE, LCSW
JENNIFER GREGG, PHD
LISA W. COYNE, PHD

New Harbinger Publications, Inc.

Publisher's Note

This publication is designed to provide accurate and authoritative information in regard to the subject matter covered. It is sold with the understanding that the publisher is not engaged in rendering psychological, financial, legal, or other professional services. If expert assistance or counseling is needed, the services of a competent professional should be sought.

NEW HARBINGER PUBLICATIONS is a registered
trademark of New Harbinger Publications, Inc.

Distributed in Canada by Raincoast Books

Copyright © 2020 by Matthew S. Boone, Jennifer Gregg, and Lisa Coyne
New Harbinger Publications, Inc.
5674 Shattuck Avenue
Oakland, CA 94609
www.newharbinger.com

Cover design by Sara Christian; Acquired by Elizabeth Hollis Hansen;
Edited by Jennifer Eastman

Library of Congress Cataloging-in-Publication Data

Names: Boone, Matthew S., author. | Gregg, Jennifer, author. | Coyne, Lisa W, author.
Title: Stop avoiding stuff : 25 microskills to face your fears and do it anyway / Matthew S. Boone,
    Jennifer Gregg, and Lisa Coyne.
Description: Oakland, CA : New Harbinger Publications, [2020] | Includes bibliographical
    references.
Identifiers: LCCN 2020022628 (print) | LCCN 2020022629 (ebook) | ISBN 9781684036059 (trade
    paperback) | ISBN 9781684036066 (pdf) | ISBN 9781684036073 (epub)
Subjects: LCSH: Fear. | Avoidance (Psychology) | Acceptance and commitment therapy. |
    Self-realization.
Classification: LCC BF575.F2 .B66 2020 (print) | LCC BF575.F2 (ebook) | DDC 152.4/6--dc23
LC record available at https://lccn.loc.gov/2020022628
LC ebook record available at https://lccn.loc.gov/2020022629

Printed in the United States of America

25   24   23

10   9   8   7   6   5   4   3   2

For my mom, who never lets the grass grow under her feet.

—MSB

For Hope and Jack, who have made my life
immeasurably more awesome.

—JAG

For Josie and Rory, my bold adventurers, with all my love.

—LWC

Contents

PART FOUR:
Shift Your View So It's Bigger Than Your Fears

PART FIVE:
Take Small Steps Toward More Engagement

PART SIX:
Get Through Avoidance Urges and Get Going: On the Spot Strategies

Welcome to This Book

Imagine that you weren't afraid of anything. What would be possible?

Think about what you could do if you weren't afraid of rejection or disapproval, vulnerability, or uncertainty. How bold would you be if you weren't scared of being sad, afraid, or hurt? Consider how amazing your life could be if you didn't fear a negative evaluation by your boss, your partner breaking up with you, your kids growing up to be terrorists, or a bear attacking you on your way home from work—all those imaginary futures our minds constantly generate. What adventure would you seek? What meaning and purpose?

If your life would be a lot different from the way it is now, this is the book for you.

Getting Stuck

Fear plays an enormous role in the ways we get stuck living lives that are stale, stagnant, or downright miserable. It's often what leads us down paths that feel safe but that, deep down, we know are wrong for us. To illustrate this point, let's meet three imaginary people who've gotten stuck in a rut, and notice how fear rules their lives.

Maria works fifteen hours a day. Some part of her knows that she should do other things—go to the gym, meet with friends, get back to throwing clay—but she can't seem to stop herself when she is in the office. She's worried that somebody else will outperform her, that she will be overlooked for a promotion, or that she will not appear good enough at her job. So she puts her head down and works endless hours, leaving the rest of her life for another day.

Armand is in a relationship that doesn't fulfill him. He often thinks about what it would be like to leave his boyfriend. But he knows his boyfriend is happy, and he can't stand how guilty he would feel if he were to leave the relationship. So he stays with him year after year, withdrawing inside and not putting his whole heart into the relationship. Meanwhile, his life feels grayer and grayer.

Ruthann has a father living in a nursing home in another state, but she can't bring herself to visit him. She loves him dearly, but when she sees his withering body and hears him ask the same questions over and over, she feels so sad. She gets absorbed in negative thinking for days on end and can't accomplish anything. So she puts off visiting him, all the while knowing that he's likely to pass away in the next few years and that she will be leveled with grief.

Can you see the common thread running through their stories? It's fear.

Living Scared

Maria, Armand, and Ruthann are living scared. They're afraid of what life might offer them if they were to change direction: work less, leave the relationship, or visit Dad in the nursing home. More specifically, they are afraid to have what might show up inside of them—the thoughts, feelings, and sensations—were they to do something different. Maria might be overwhelmed with an urge to get back to work. Armand might be racked with guilt. And Ruthann might be overcome with sadness.

When we say they are "afraid," we don't necessarily mean that they are experiencing real fear: racing heart, elevated blood pressure, an urge to fight or flee. We don't mean necessarily that they are anxious either. They may or may not experience the worried thoughts, tension, and stomach butterflies that make up anxiety.

When we say "afraid," "fear," and "scared," we are using these terms in two ways: yes, sometimes we are using them in a technical way to talk about the actual experience of fear and anxiety. But we are also using them in the way that they are used in popular culture when people say things like "afraid of failing" or "fear of intimacy" or "scared to be alone." What ties the technical way of talking about fear with the more colloquial, casual way of talking, is that they both imply avoidance: staying away from things that are uncomfortable or unfamiliar. What Maria, Armand, and Ruthann are doing is avoiding.

Avoiding the Hard Stuff

Let's be clear: saying they are avoiding is not a judgment. It's simply a description of their behavior. And we all have this behavior to some degree: our ancestors, the ones who populated the African savanna hundreds of thousands of years ago, survived by staying away from situations that made them feel fear. So we all came by this avoidance honestly. It's a habit we've been practicing, possibly without our awareness, for most of our lives. And because it's old and engrained, it can be a tricky habit to break, especially when it has become so prevalent in your life that you have become stuck like Maria, Armand, and Ruthann.

So how can you stop living scared and avoiding stuff that's hard? You picked up this book, so you are aware of what's happening. If you feel changing course would be worthwhile, you're surely wondering how you can actually make that change.

Ending Avoidance and Facing Your Fears

People often talk of courage as if it's something we have inside of us—a feeling or drive that propels us forward. If we are afraid, then what we need is courage to help us get over it. But how do we get that courage? It seems like something we should have, so when we don't, it feels completely elusive.

There's a more useful way to look at courage, one that makes courage available to anyone, no matter how afraid they feel or how entrenched they are in avoiding and living scared. When courage is regarded as a skill we can learn, practice, and, to some degree, master, so much more becomes possible.

You can learn to stop avoiding, face your fears, and show up to life as a full participant, even when doing so scares the heck out of you. We'd like to offer you a way to fully engage your life, however it unfolds—not just the stuff that happens in your life (relationships, jobs, vacations, births, deaths, hardships), but also the stuff that occurs inside you while you're living it (joy, sadness, excitement, boredom, guilt, anxiety).

So what does it mean to stop avoiding and face your fears? In a nutshell, it means taking part in life as a full participant, whether that means fully engaging in the boring book your toddler wants you to read to her yet again (even though your work email is piling up) or wholly embracing the sadness that arises as you notice that she's getting older and won't always be the baby you love so much. It means facing stuff that sucks— boredom, sadness, whatever—and *doing it anyway.*

This requires that you spend some time considering how you want to be in any moment, knowing that all you can control is your actions. You can't control other people. You can't force the world to fit into your mold. But you can decide what's important to you and live that out.

How to Use This Book

This book is broken down into twenty-five short chapters. Each one describes a microskill: an effective way of relating to your thoughts, feelings, and circumstances that is based on scientific wisdom. Many of the skills are illustrated with stories from our lives. When that happens, you'll see a note about who's talking— Jen, Lisa, or Matt. Each one of these microskills can be put into practice right away to reduce avoidance and maximize your engagement in life. We've made it especially easy to get started by ending each chapter with a "teeny tiny practice" you can try immediately. But you can put the microskill into practice in any way you like.

Each chapter is somewhat independent of the others, but they are all related. The idea is that you can open up to any page, at any time, and glean something meaningful from what you read in a short amount of time. In essence, it's a book you can take to the bathroom with you.

You can also read this book from beginning to end, which might have the most impact. Though the chapters are independent, they make up a coherent whole, with each microskill building on the others to offer you a method for organizing life in a meaningful way, so that you can actually know what it's like, in your experience, to feel your fear and stop avoiding.

Even though you can dip into this book at any spot, do read the full introduction, because it will orient you to how we think about behavior, especially unnecessary avoidance and control, the heart of what can make life narrow, empty, and downright sucky. So read the introduction, then jump to any chapter you like or start at Microskill 1 and see what happens. Your life is waiting for you to join it.

Will This Book Help You?

We don't know for sure. That may sound funny, but it's true. Few self-help books are subjected to the kind of science that would show whether or not they actually help. We have not conducted research on this book, at least not yet, so we're not going to make any claims. That would just be dumb. And unscientific.

However, what we are offering you is definitely grounded in science. The method in this book is based on acceptance and commitment therapy (ACT), a behavior therapy that has been shown to be effective for a wide range of problems in over three hundred well-designed studies. We've also drawn a few concepts from positive psychology, a field of study that focuses on enhancing your life through meaning and purpose, which also has a deep research base. So this book may not be "evidence-based" as a standalone self-help book, but the ideas contained herein certainly are evidence-based. So we are pretty confident it will make a difference if you adopt these microskills. At the back of this book is a resources section that lists some books with similar themes that have been subjected to research, in case you're curious.

We hope that every page offers you something important that can make a small difference in your life.

Meet Your Avoidance

To live courageously—to stop avoiding stuff and do what matters—we invite you to first learn how your avoidance works. It is essential to be able to notice and understand what you are doing when you are doing it.

One simple way to think about this is to remember this phrase: *You do, you get.* For example, in the following scenarios, what you get from avoiding stuff is in italics:

- When you stay home, *you don't have to worry about what folks will think of you at that party.*

- When you feel anxious, you have a drink and *feel less anxious.*

- When you feel sad, you start scrolling on your phone, and *sadness fades into the background.*

- When you feel hurt or vulnerable, you yell at your spouse and *feel a small release of the anger.*

The stuff you *get* is important—it determines, at least in part, whether you do the thing again or whether you stop. If drinking in social situations eases your feelings of awkwardness or discomfort, you are more likely to continue drinking. If avoiding the party reduces your anxiety, you are more likely to avoid in other ways—like not returning your friends' calls, not answering those emailed invitations, and so on.

Everything You Do Makes Sense

This may seem really basic, but it's fundamental to understanding human behavior. What you do works for you in some way; people avoid stuff because, to some degree, it works. What this means is that everything you do makes sense. People don't do stuff that doesn't work. The tricky part is whether stuff works the way you *think* it does and whether it has other consequences. More on that in a bit.

Can you see how avoidance might work really well in some situations? When you avoid, you get something—often a temporary reprieve from feeling uncomfortable. When you procrastinate doing your taxes, you get to put off the anxiety that shows up when you face your financial life. If you don't speak up in a work meeting, you get temporary freedom from worrying what your colleagues think of your ideas. But, of course, there are costs of these behaviors, and anxiety and worry don't go away for good.

Triggers: What Happens Before You Do What You Do

What tells you when, where, and how to avoid stuff? Something has to set the stage for all humans to avoid, for us to *do*—or *not do*—and subsequently *get*. You might call the stuff that tells you what to do and when to do it a "trigger." Triggers can be anything at all—a feeling, a thought, a memory, an absence, a longing for something. We'll use the same examples for this list and put the triggers in italics.

- *You imagine how awful you will feel when you don't fit in at the party,* so you stay home, and you don't have to worry about what folks will think of you at that party.

- *You feel anxious that your boss criticized you today,* so you have a drink and feel less anxious.

- *You think, "Why do I always have to be the one who reaches out to people? Why don't they reach out to me?"* You feel sad. You start scrolling, and the sadness fades into the background.

- *Your son talked back to you today, and he's out of control;* you're hurt and vulnerable, so you yell at your spouse.

Notice that most of these triggers involve something going on inside of you, like a thought or feeling, even if they arise in response to something going on outside of you. We are thinking and feeling organisms. It's too simple to say that thoughts and feelings *cause* our actions. (Just remember the last time your mind told you to eat another scoop of ice cream and you didn't.) But what goes on inside of us has an enormous influence on what we do.

Avoidance Is About Control

Once you have gotten the hang of understanding how your avoidance works, you can take control of it and simply stop avoiding. Right? Well, it turns out that control is part of the problem.

Avoidance is about control. When we avoid, we are staying away from discomfort. If you never go back and get your degree, you never have to think, "Am I smart enough to do this?" If you never take that ballroom dance class, you'll never have to feel clumsy and inept. If you never ask out the lovely woman who works at the library, you'll never have to feel your racing heart and your flushed face—not to mention what you might feel if she says no. You get to exert a measure of control over all of that uncomfortable stuff by staying away from the situations that might evoke it. But controlling, especially controlling through avoiding, doesn't really work as well as we think it does. Read on.

How Much Control Do We Really Have?

Humans love control. We love it! What's not to love? Control lets us choose what to do with our day. It allows us to do stuff we like and avoid stuff we don't. Like this:

- If you don't like soy vanilla lattes, you don't order them.

- If you don't want your house painted red, you head off to the hardware store and pick out a lovely blue.

- If you don't like a comment someone posted on your Instagram, you can simply delete it.

- If you're anxious and your heart is racing, you can just choose not to feel that. Just slow your heart down. Voila!

- If you think, *Wow, I am really pissed off at my spouse,* you can just put that thought right out of your mind and not feel mad anymore.

- If you feel depressed, you can just replace those miserable negative thoughts with positive ones and snap out of it. Just be happy!

Right? If at this point you're thinking, *Wait, I'm not sure I can do those last few things,* then congratulations! You are human.

Your experience has probably told you that these last three things are impossible.

Control on the Outside Versus Control on the Inside

There's a difference between controlling stuff *outside* of our heads (in the world) versus *inside* our heads. For example, you might be able to delete that nasty Instagram comment on your phone, but it doesn't necessarily get it out of your head. In the same way:

- If you're feeling anxious about work, you might distract yourself by scrolling social media and just procrastinate. It probably makes you feel a little better in the short term, but does it dispel your anxiety for good or make it easier to get those overdue tasks done?

- When you are sad and tell yourself to put on a happy face, it doesn't necessarily fix it. It might make you feel better for a short while (or not), but does it make the sadness disappear?

- Ever try to change your negative thoughts by thinking positive thoughts? Maybe you have sticky-note sayings all over your house and desk, or maybe you give pep talks to the mirror. Are you satisfied with the results? Do the negative thoughts just move on, never to return?

We're pretty sure you answered no to those questions. Notice how much of what you try to control is about not feeling bad stuff. Or not thinking bad stuff. That's what avoiding stuff usually is: an effort to control uncomfortable feelings inside of us by staying away from the circumstances that give rise to them.

It's not that we have no influence over what shows up inside of us. We've all had the experience of pushing away a thought or feeling for a moment in order to get things done. It's just that trying to control the stuff that comes from your head and your heart is just not as reliably successful as we expect it to be. And the more intense or meaningful that stuff is—if it's the anger you feel about getting laid off, the memory of a time when you felt intense shame, or the fear you feel about leaving a toxic relationship—the harder it is.

Control: Is It a Feature or a Bug?

But if controlling the stuff between our ears doesn't work the way we want it to, why do we keep trying to do it? Is it a bug in our programming? If you use some of these control strategies for stuff you don't want to feel or think, you're not alone. In fact, all humans do this at some point or another. It's an extension of something we've evolved to do over the course of our history as a species: avoiding threat.

Humans are at the top of the food chain. But we don't have sharp teeth or claws. We don't even run very fast. And yet, we are arguably the world's most successful predator—for better or worse. We've traded in our pointy bits for the most powerful weapon of all—our cerebral cortex. It's an amazing feature that allows us to do all sorts of abstract thinking and planning and problem solving. It allows us to think about the past and future and to learn indirectly from mental rules rather than from direct experience. And thank goodness! Otherwise we'd have to get knocked down by a car in order to learn how to look both ways before crossing a street.

Think about that for a second: animals learn from their experience. Your dog discovers that sitting is a good thing because she gets treats and praise. She learns to avoid the cat because she gets scratched. But humans can learn in many other ways as well, most of them involving our big, awesome brains. So rather than biting, clawing, or running to protect ourselves, we have a big brain whose number one job is to help us avoid threat. It's definitely a feature rather than a bug.

The only problem is that what we perceive as *threats* are different from when we were living during the stone age. It's that pesky inside-outside problem again.

Unintended Consequences

The problem is not just that control doesn't work the way we hope it will. There are other consequences as well. The more we try to tighten our control, the less attention we can pay to other things outside in the world. The more we try to avoid, the stronger the need to avoid gets. And the smaller and smaller our lives become.

Think back again to the three people we met earlier— Maria, Armand, and Ruthann. Maria works all the time because slowing down brings up an intense fear of failure. Armand doesn't want to have the guilt that shows up if he considers leaving his partner. And Ruthann avoids the sadness of her father's decline by never visiting. Their lives have become unworkable because they are treating thoughts and feelings like saber-toothed tigers.

What's the alternative? That's what this book is about. You've heard the expression, "feel the fear and do it anyway"? That's what we want to teach you. We want to show you how to approach the things you would rather avoid, get more skillful at encountering the thoughts and feelings you don't want to have, and start doing more of what brings you toward a vital and meaningful life. It sounds like a tall order, but it's totally doable. Especially with many teeny tiny efforts.

Throughout this book, there are teeny tiny practices that we will invite you to try. You'll learn best if you do them, so we encourage you to keep a small notebook to write responses down.

Grab your notebook and write down something that you struggle with. It should be something that gives you a little bit of a stomach ache to think of. Don't worry—nobody will see what you write down, so write down something real.

1. List the main things you've tried to fix, solve, or eliminate this struggle. These could include one or more of the following:

    *   problem solving

    *   trying to figure out "why?"

    *   criticizing yourself

    *   worrying

    *   criticizing others

    *   thinking *if only* …

    *   thinking *what if* …

    *   imagining big changes in your life

    *   imagining you weren't alive

Whatever you've tried, write it down. They can be things we usually label as "unhealthy" as well as things we usually label as "healthy."

2. Then circle everything that works in the short term, at least a little bit, to pull you away from the struggle.

3. Put a star by everything that works in the long term to pull you away from the struggle.

4. Finally, underline everything that brings you closer to a vital, vibrant, and more meaningful life.

What do you notice? Write your observations down in your journal.

Here's what we hope you notice: that almost everything works a little bit in the short term. Remember: *you do, you get*. We wouldn't do these things if they didn't have at least some kind of minor impact on what we think and feel.

We also hope you notice that most, if not all, of them don't make your thoughts and feelings go away in the long term. Whatever you do, "healthy" or "unhealthy," you will likely still experience painful thoughts and uncomfortable emotions. That's just how we are built.

We also want you to notice that some behaviors don't make your feelings go away, but they do help you build the life you want to lead.

Finally—and this insight is a big deal—consider how sometimes your behavior can be about trying to avoid and control your internal experiences, and other times it can be about building a life you want. That's a really important difference to notice. What we'd like is for your behavior to begin to be less and less about ineffective and unnecessary control strategies. Instead, more and more, you'll act to build that meaningful life you want. That's the overall aim of all the microskills that follow. So get started by reading on!

PART ONE

Build Awareness of the Moment to Seize the Moment

The first step to stopping avoidance and facing your fears is building awareness. One of the most effective ways to do this is to be mindful. You've heard of mindfulness, right? It's pretty popular right now. Mindfulness is recommended as an antidote to just about everything: stress, anxiety, pain, overwork—you name it. If you do an image search on your favorite search engine, you'll get a bazillion pictures of beautiful people sitting in the lotus position, looking blissful and serene.

Those images don't always square with people's lived experience of mindfulness. For example, one basic mindfulness practice is to pay attention to your breath as it goes in and out. If you've ever tried it, you've noticed that it can be really hard. Your mind drifts off almost immediately. And you have to bring it back many, many times. The experience is rarely blissful and serene.

The truth is, mindfulness isn't really an *antidote* to anything. It's not about being calm or peaceful, though those feelings can arise when you are practicing it. Mindfulness is about being present: simply noticing what's there, right in front of you, in the here and now. If you can do that, you can learn to *respond* rather than *react*.

Reacting is what we usually do, as we habitually follow our urges, engage in old, tired habits, and, most important, avoid stuff. Responding means making a choice: seeing what's going on, as it happens, and deciding what you want to do about it. So if you feel anxious about moving forward, *you* decide whether you move forward, not your anxiety. If you feel a strong urge to avoid, you—and not your urge—decide what to do.

The microskills here in part 1 encourage you to be mindful, but they start you off in a really easy place. There's no cushion to sit on, no lotus position to pretzel into, and no blissful smile to adopt. In Microskill 1, we just ask that you get curious about what's going on outside of you (your circumstances, your environment, the actions of other people) and inside of you (your thoughts, feelings, sensations, urges, and memories). That's all.

We then encourage you in Microskill 2 to cultivate what we call the "observer's perspective." It's another simple way to be mindful without putting on yoga pants or burning incense. Taking this perspective means not only noticing what's going on in the moment, but also *noticing that you are noticing.* It's developing a sense that there is a part of you that is distinct from what you are experiencing. From that perspective, all the thoughts and feelings you try to avoid can't harm you. They are what you experience, not what you *are.* Over time, you begin to understand—in your gut—that pain, however sucky, is only temporary. With this understanding, moving forward—even when it's unpleasant—becomes more possible.

In Microskill 3, we finish by teaching a simple, formal mindfulness practice, the kind in which you set aside some time and close your eyes. Even though the *idea* of sitting mindfulness practice is trendy, the *practice* is still one of the best ways to get to know yourself, so that you can get to know your tendency to avoid stuff and, from a place of responding—not reacting—do what matters.

MICROSKILL 1 Get Curious About the World

One way to let go of avoidance is to pay attention, on purpose, to the present. This is mindfulness. We know, we know—mindfulness sometimes scares people off, because it seems kind of daunting. But there is a less strenuous way to develop mindfulness skills than sitting down on a cushion and practicing silent stillness. We're going to teach you a way to be mindful even if the idea of meditation makes you remember some laundry you've been meaning to do.

In application, mindfulness is just bringing your attention to the present, and then, at some point, noticing that it has wandered away, and then noticing where it has wandered, and then bringing it back to the present moment. And then repeating that nine to ten million times.

Mindfulness is a practice; it is not a steady state. We like to think of it as an intentional, occasional state of paying attention to what is going on, on purpose and without judgment, and then a whole lot of forgetting to do that—and returning to it when you remember again.

How to Not Practice Mindfulness

The first time I (Jen) decided to practice mindfulness, I was in my early twenties, and I ended up on a weekend silent retreat with a bunch of meditators. In retrospect, maybe this was not the best idea—to jump right in to a multiday silent retreat—but generating great ideas was not my thing at the time, so I assumed it would be fun and easy.

When I sat down to meditate, the inside of my head sounded a lot like this: *Okay, what am I supposed to do here? I'm pretty sure I'm doing it wrong … yep, definitely doing it wrong. Can you do meditation wrong? Isn't that being too judgmental or something? I'm sure you can do it wrong, and I'm sure I am. …* [peeking one eye open] *Everybody else seems to be doing it right. How do they know what to do? Why can't I do this? Argh!*

That is pretty much what the whole weekend sounded like, with (very infrequent) moments that I felt like I was doing it "right" that sounded like, *Oh my gosh, I'm the best meditator in the whole world. I've totally got this. Wait—where did it go?*

An Easier Path to Mindfulness

We said before that there is an easier way to access mindfulness than sitting down on a cushion. It involves being curious about what is happening *now.* Curiosity allows us to be present and aware in a relaxed, easy way, because it doesn't have an invest-ment in a particular result or outcome—it's just checking it out.

This curiosity can be focused on things going on *outside* of you right now (in your environment, what you are doing) or *inside* of you (your thoughts, feelings, bodily sensations, or urges).

CURIOSITY ABOUT THE EXTERNAL

First let's talk about getting curious about things outside of you. Try this experiment: Notice what you are doing right now. Notice where you are, who is around, what activity or sounds you notice around you. Imagine you are seeing yourself from the outside. What do you see? What sounds can you hear? Smells? Sights?

Do you notice that doing this brought you out of your think-ing and into your life for just a minute?

There are lots of reasons why being curious about what is going on outside of you can be useful. It lets you see how the world influences you and how you influence the world. For example, if we take the example of Maria, who was working all the time in order to avoid her fear of failure, more curiosity might have allowed her to notice that she was alienated from her col-leagues and her friends had stopped inviting her to events, figur-ing she was too busy.

Second, being curious about the world around you may improve your quality of life. In fact, there is some evidence that when people are mentally engaged with the activities they are doing, they tend to be happier than when they are lost in thought, no matter what the content of those thoughts (Killingsworth & Gilbert, 2010). While having "being happy" or "having happy feelings" as a goal can backfire and lead to avoidance of tough stuff, it's cool that people who are engaged with their surroundings tend to like their life better.

CURIOSITY ABOUT THE INTERNAL

Being curious can also give you a clearer perspective on the stuff going on inside your skin. If you can do that, you can notice what gives rise to avoidance that's not working for you—procrastinating, not being honest with your partner, letting your mother's calls go to voicemail—and face whatever fear is there, and then take the opportunity to do things differently.

Applying this same curiosity to the stuff going on inside has clear benefits. Curiosity allows you to see your thoughts as what they are—thoughts! It allows you to see bodily sensations as bodily sensations, emotions as emotions, and memories as memories.

Try it out: What do you notice going on inside you right now? What does the air feel like on your skin? What thoughts are you having right now? What story are you telling yourself? Can you see that they are just thoughts? What sensations do you notice in your body?

Becoming aware of things inside your skin can sometimes be more difficult than noticing outside things, but regularly turning your curiosity inward is a great way to build this skill.

As you get better at connecting to curiosity in tough moments, you will build more skills at mindfully being aware of the present moment (without the need of a cushion!), which will allow you to more easily face your fears and move forward in your life.

Practicing Curiosity, In and Out

This week, write down an intention in your notebook (and maybe some reminders—a sticky note on your monitor, an alarm on your phone) to practice curiosity. Notice your surroundings at different times of the day; be curious about what thoughts you're having, what sensations you can notice, what you're doing, and what magical thing your mind is telling you is about to happen next.

Observe All the Comings and Goings

Once you have gotten curious about the world and your inner experience, you can enhance that curiosity by noticing the part of you that is being curious. Noticing the noticer. Observing the observer. Trippy, right? Noticing that there is a person noticing that there's a person noticing.

Here's why this is important: if you are the person noticing the noticing, then the thing you are noticing—by definition—can't actually harm you. It can hurt like crazy. You can wish it wasn't there or would go away. But it can't *harm* you, no matter how much it seems like it can.

If your thoughts and feelings can't harm you, then the need to avoid them goes down dramatically. In essence, learning the skill of observing the observer helps you build up your "handling hard moments" muscles by no longer making fear, sadness, guilt, shame, or vulnerability things that must be avoided.

How to Observe the Observer

When we are the observer, we can see thoughts arising, persisting for some period of time, and then passing away without our needing to do anything. The trick to being the observer is to pay attention to the *process* of the thoughts, rather than the *content*. Easier said than done, but sometimes being the observer allows you to stand back just far enough to be able to face the fears, overcome avoidance, and do what you care about in the situation.

TRY THIS: Think about something that hurts or scares you. Maybe a time you were fired or dumped or had someone treat you like crap. Or your fear that this will happen in the future. Just pick one. When you think about it, what do you notice? What sensations do you feel in your body? What thoughts? Emotions?

Now—who just noticed those things? It's you. You noticed all those things. When you notice that it's you doing the noticing, we call that "observing the observer."

When I (Jen) think about a time that I was dumped in college, I notice that my chest feels a little tight, with a kind of ache in it. I notice that I feel a little sad and hurt. I notice that I have lots of judgments and thoughts about how unfair it was and how badly it was done. Who was noticing this? Me.

When I notice that it's me noticing, the experience changes a little. It definitely still hurts a little to think about, but if I notice the thoughts, feelings, and body sensations that go with it, I can kind of notice that I'm noticing those. My thoughts and feelings might change, but I stay the same.

Observing Can Prevent Disastrous Reactions

I (Jen) was once talking to a friend, when, out of nowhere, she said something critical about my infant daughter. It caught me off guard and felt like a punch in the gut (especially in my perpetually sleep-deprived state at the time). I guess she just assumed I had the same judgment about my daughter, but I definitely didn't, and—mama bear that I can be—I was pretty offended by what she said.

Unlike most times I had been in this situation before, this time I was able to notice my reactivity and observe it. It sounded a little like, *Roooaaarrr! How dare you insult my little baby?!* My heart was beating fast, and my chest was all squeezy.

I kept noticing it for an eternity (or, actually, probably about three minutes), and pretty soon I was able to notice that I was noticing. And, remarkably, the more I noticed that I was noticing, the easier it was to wait until I could respond to my friend from a state other than my mama-bear reactivity.

What was cool about this experience wasn't that I was able to notice what was happening—we can do that most of the time—but rather that I was able to drop into this perspective in a moment I didn't *want* to be reactive. What I wanted to do in that moment was give her the benefit of the doubt, but it felt impossible to do. I was able to do it anyway, because it let me wait until I could to *respond*, rather than *react*. I was able to have her help me understand where she was coming from (which allowed me to see that she had meant something slightly different from what I had heard), rather than blowing up.

Pain, as Sucky as It Is, Is Temporary

Another fact about difficult experiences is that every sensation or experience we observe changes eventually. No matter how terrible the psychological experience you are having, it is not going to last forever. This can shift you into taking an observer perspective. Even if you're *really* upset about something, eventually you are going to want to go have a sandwich. And, if you think about the things you were really worried about a month ago, chances are you are not even thinking about some of them today.

Taking an observer perspective allows you to notice when the feeling has changed—so you don't need to avoid it—and allows you to focus on other aspects of your life. What if you could say to yourself, *Oh, look—I'm feeling scared about changing jobs, and I feel the fear in my chest, and if the fear could talk, it would say, "Don't be crazy. What if this all falls apart?!" But I know that that thought shows up when I'm taking risks, and this is a risk that matters to me, so I'm just going to observe the fear and the thoughts until the next thought or feeling comes along.* Imagine how many things you could do.

Notice Who's Noticing

Take a minute to sit down with your notebook and notice, just like you did in Microskill 1, your internal and external experience right now.

1. What is going on around you right now? Are there sounds? If you stop reading and look around, what do you see? Then close your eyes and notice what the air feels like on your skin. Notice the feel of the air coming in and out of your nose. Can you smell anything? What thoughts are you having? Write down everything you're experiencing.

2. Now notice that it's you who is noticing these things. That there is an observer who is observing all of these experiences.

3. Finally, add to the written description of your experience a description of what it's like to notice these things. It's okay if it feels hard to do or if you don't have much to write; the goal is to just practice noticing that you're noticing.

MICROSKILL 3 Deepen Awareness of Your Inner Experience

Now that you're bringing curiosity to your internal and external experience and observing the observer, we are going to share a more formal practice of mindfulness—the kind meditators use—because it continues to build these skills.

Benefits of Mindfulness Meditation

The advantage to the cushion—or to the act of sitting down purposefully to meditate—is that it allows you to observe your experience in slow motion. It is hard to be mindful while you're busy with work or other tasks (let alone interacting with other people, which is when our mindfulness slips away). Meditation provides a space without distractions and without things you need to focus on—you can just practice.

Goals of Mindfulness Practice

The goal of mindfulness practice is not to eliminate thinking. It is to bring gentle awareness to the process of your thinking; it helps you step outside of your thinking for a second, notice that it is taking place, begin to notice the patterns, and notice that there is a present right here all the time that exists outside of that system.

It is a little amazing, if you think about it, that we go through our lives looking at the world through our thoughts without ever really noticing the present moment most of the time.

Default Mode Network

When we're not actively engaged in a task, activity, or experience, we typically say that our mind "wanders." This is a useful metaphor, but it is also useful to think about what is actually happening when we're not engaged with our present experience. Scientists describe this "wandering" as engaging the Default Mode Network (DMN) in your brain. It turns out that a large network of connected brain regions wake up when your mind is wandering (usually to positive or negative thoughts about yourself, other people, or past or future experiences) and goes quiet when your mind is focused on something in the present.

It is easy to step out of the DMN when you're rock climbing or putting together a puzzle—these are times when your mind naturally is engaged with the present moment. It is more difficult, however, to train your mind to stay out of the DMN when you are waiting for the bus or attempting to be more present in your life. The best way to build your awareness of your inner experience is to practice this in a formal and structured way. To sit down and intentionally practice bringing your focus back to the present on purpose—focusing on your breath or *noticing* your thoughts rather than being pulled in by them—over and over again. Let's see what happens with your own DMN with the following exercise:

1. Find a seat somewhere comfortable. Take a few moments to let your noticing self check in with your body and see how it feels in the chair. Notice the points of contact between your body and the chair; notice the feeling of support or warmth. Let your noticing self briefly scan your body for any tension you might be holding. Do you want to be holding yourself tightly? If so, great. If not, you may choose to loosen up that hold. Take a few moments to notice parts of your body that you don't normally notice—like the top of your head. Or your left elbow. Your right earlobe.

2. Then check out your mental wallpaper—your thoughts. Notice them as they shift and change, come and go. As you notice each thought, allow a brief pause, and cast your attention toward the emotions each thought leaves in its wake. See if you can notice their intensity or mildness; see if you can notice where they reside inside your skin. For example, if you are feeling anxious, does that show up in the pit of your stomach? Or does it live more in your neck and shoulders?

3. Notice your body breathing. See if you can notice, without doing anything to change it, your body drawing in air when it needs it and then letting it go. Notice your chest rising and falling as your lungs expand and contract. Notice that your body has been doing this activity since the day you were born, whether you were aware of it or not. As you do this, simply notice what it is like to bring your awareness gently to this internal landscape, rather than speeding past it or avoiding it entirely.

Was this a bit of a challenge? If so, you're not alone in that. Most of us are busy getting on with our days instead of spending time exploring our interior worlds. In fact, busyness may have become our modus operandi, almost as though we are sleepwalking through our lives. But there's a cost to this: if we live on autopilot, we lose our ability to pause and choose our next steps and our direction.

How Will This Help Me Resist Avoidance?

Sometimes it can feel like the things we do are simply automatic. They just, well, *happen*. Sometimes they even happen outside of our awareness! But once you have developed a practice of noticing—first, your five senses; next, your observing self; and now, your internal landscape—this is going to open up a really interesting state in which you can pause and choose what to do next.

It's sort of like more actively living your life, rather than passively letting life happen to you. So you might have the thought that your actions or responses are automatic—and certainly they may feel that way—and also you can shape the skill of awareness so that you have much greater choice in the matter.

In addition, there is a vast amount of information available to us inside our skins. As we mentioned, emotions, thoughts, and physiological sensations are *information*. They help direct us to the things that really matter to us; they can inform how we proceed in our relationships, work, or other pursuits. If we avoid or speed past these, we lose out. We will talk about this more in Microskill 4.

TEENY TINY PRACTICE
Pausing to Notice Your Breath and Body

Each day, take a few moments to practice the exercise in this chapter. It doesn't have to be for hours at a time or in a way that overwhelms your system, but setting aside time each day to practice mindful meditation will build your ability to observe and learn from your experience.

PART TWO

Feel Your Feelings Without Running Away

Avoidance is about controlling uncomfortable stuff inside you. If you avoid a situation that evokes a feeling of anxiety, you temporarily minimize that anxiety. But avoiding doesn't make anxiety go away for good. Anxiety is still likely to show up again, no matter how much you try to stay away from it. Sadly, there's no magic wand to make the anxiety—or whatever discomfort you are feeling—go away. The alternative is to learn to feel what there is to feel, even when it's uncomfortable.

"Feeling what you feel" can seem a little bit abstract. It makes more sense if you understand what emotions are. Emotions are your natural, evolutionarily shaped responses to the world. Emotions tell you when something is pleasurable, fun, scary, or threatening. If we didn't have emotions, we wouldn't have that information. Think of the last time your mind really convinced you, all by itself, that you were having a good time. I'm guessing you can't. Our intellect doesn't convince us we are happy, sad, afraid, angry, or whatever. It's our emotions!

In Microskill 4, you will learn to map out the components of your emotions—the thoughts, sensations, and urges that make them up—so you can get to know them a little more deeply. When you do so, they become less mysterious and less scary. They become experiences we might move toward rather than away from. Microskill 5 continues that work by offering a simple practice of observing and describing emotions.

Moving toward discomfort, especially when it serves something important to you, is called willingness, which we address in Microskill 6. Willingness entails embracing whatever shows up inside you, as well as what happens in your life, without running away. It's about letting go of what you can't control, putting your energy into what you can—and knowing the difference.

So if you find yourself avoiding, you can note that the discomfort you are trying to control by avoiding is not the enemy. You can actually get closer to it by observing it, allowing it to be there, and even breathing into and around it in a mindful way, which we introduce in Microskill 7. When you do this, you transform your relationship with it. Suddenly the discomfort is less of a barrier. You can stop protecting yourself from it and move your feet in a new direction, even when you'd rather avoid.

Understand How Your Emotions Work

You've just been dumped. You're ugly-crying, the kind that contorts your face into a swollen fun-house-mirror version of itself. You're sobbing so hard you think you might throw up. You don't even notice the snot streaming from your nose. It's times like these that make you wonder, *Why the hell do we have emotions, anyway? What good are they?*

Emotions Are Information, Not Enemies

Emotions become less mysterious and, frankly, less embarrassing when we think of them as information, not enemies. Long before our ancestors had language beyond grunts and gestures to communicate with themselves and one another, they needed good information to mediate their experience of the world.

They needed information from their bodies. They needed to know they were hungry in order to maintain their health and energy, so their bodies sent them hunger signals. They needed to protect themselves from sharp objects and roaring fires, so their bodies sent them pain signals. And they needed to feel aroused to get down to the business of procreating and propagating the species, so their bodies sent them sexual arousal signals.

They also needed information beyond just pain or pleasure. Their survival depended on more than just eating and copulating. They needed emotional information: anxiety to know that there might be a threat and fear to tell them to run away, anger to motivate them to protect themselves when fighting was the only option, sadness to signal a loss and motivate them to stick with one another, and shame to tell them when they had strayed from the norms of their community, something that could leave them more vulnerable to threat.

Aren't you glad you're not a cave person? Life on the ancient African savanna must have sucked! Threats everywhere! And the coffee was probably horrible.

These evolutionary explanations don't tell the entire story—there are volumes of science that drill down to the nitty-gritty—but they do a pretty good job of making emotions make sense. The bottom line is that we needed emotions then, and we need them now.

Emotions in Contemporary Life

Our modern-day struggle with emotions begins to make some sense in the context of our relatively cushy lives when we consider that we tend to respond to painful emotions as if they are signaling *real* threats. But most of the threats we perceive are symbolic—we are not actually on the edge of survival at all times, needing to be ready to fight or flee.

What do we mean by "symbolic"? Let's say you feel angry after someone cuts you off in traffic. You bang your fist against the steering wheel, and, if it's a really bad day, get all up on the bumper of the dude who cut you off.

Anger tends to arise in response to a threat. (Fear does, too.) What's the threat here? Sure, there is a literal threat to your safety; driving a car is a dangerous thing to do, so why make it more dangerous by driving like a maniac? But there may be things that are only "threatening" to some part of you that has nothing to do with the integrity of your body. These are symbolic threats. There could be a threat to your ego (*Who does this guy think he is, and why does he think he's entitled to just cut me off?*). Or a threat to your implicit rules about how people are supposed to behave (*That's not how you're supposed to act!*). Or maybe to your peace of mind (*I didn't sign up for a demolition derby, pencil-neck!*). It could be anything your mind creates.

Our capacity to respond to this stuff as if it's literally threatening has a big influence on our tendency to avoid the hard stuff. Say you want to ask your boss for a raise, and you imagine how bad you might feel if she said no. Therefore, you avoid having the conversation. You're treating that imagined "bad" feeling as something to stay away from, like our ancestors stayed away from tigers. Instead, that feeling—whether it's sadness, anger, or shame—could be thought of as the cost of living life fully. If you're going to take risks, you're going to feel uncomfortable. Avoiding the possibility of it just narrows your life into something small.

Map Your Emotion

When a strong emotion arises, and you feel (A) puzzled by it, (B) tempted to run away from it, or (C) an urge to criticize yourself for having it, one of the simplest things you can do is to map out its components.

Emotions have three parts: thoughts, feelings, and urges. Thoughts are the words, sounds, and pictures that go through your mind. Feelings are the sensations in your body. And urges are your inclinations to do something. With this in mind, ask yourself these questions:

- What's the situation? (For example, I want to ask my boss for a raise.)

- What am I feeling in my body? (My face is flushed; my hands are tense.)

- What are my thoughts? ("What if she thinks I'm full of myself? What if she says no?")

- What is my action urge? (Avoid talking about it.)

- Does following my action urge take me in the direction of what I care about? (No, it just makes me feel underappreciated and resentful, and I'll have to drive my old clunker forever.)

Mapping your reaction this way can offer you a few important benefits. First, it's a way of responding to your emotions without getting so wrapped up in them that they start running your life. Second, it's a way to watch them without criticizing them or pushing them away, which can work in the short term, but often leads to a rebound. Finally, in the interest of breaking free from avoidance, you need tools to help you encounter the emotions that will show up as you face your fears. Mapping your emotions is a simple way to have the emotion and move forward, even if that emotion is tugging you in the other direction.

So remember, when something shows up inside of you that you don't like and want to get away from, map it out: situation, feeling, thought, urge. Then ask yourself, *Do I want to go where this takes me?*

Feel Emotions—Don't Fight or Feed Them

We get this message that allowing ourselves to feel our emotions, rather than pushing them away, is good for us. It's like eating our broccoli. But no one ever tells us how. What do they mean by *feel your emotions*? How the hell are we supposed to just feel them?

Actually, feeling doesn't seem to be the real problem. The problem may be feeling them all day and night. Or punching holes in the wall. Or curling up into a ball and muttering to ourselves.

What Feeling Your Emotions Really Means

It turns out that the instruction to *just feel your emotions* hinges on the word "just." All that other stuff—stewing in them, yelling about them, endlessly journaling about them, expressing them to your buddy over three or four or fourteen beers—is stuff we do in addition to feeling them. Some of these responses are useful. Some of them are not.

These behaviors can actually be about avoiding your emotions, as well as avoiding your life. Have you ever found yourself having trouble letting go of some injustice and moving on? Maybe you felt wronged by someone's misinterpretation of what you said, you were passed over for that promotion, or you lost a person or pet who was precious to you. You may have noticed that long past the usefulness of thinking and talking about it all the time, you were still thinking and talking about it all the time. You weren't moving forward and facing the scariness of building a new relationship, rebuilding a career, or engaging with life in the face of your pain.

We're not condemning thinking and talking about your emotions. We're suggesting that all that activity doesn't always equal fully feeling your emotions. Remember when we told you that *when you do, you get*? When you dwell on something bad, you are getting some kind of payoff: maybe a sense of righteousness (*Look at this injustice!*), self-validation (*This explains how bad I feel*), or self-protection (*If I keep thinking about this, it won't happen again*). Those are important payoffs, especially in the beginning. But eventually you may be avoiding the discomfort of really contacting the pain.

You may discover that the only way to move on with your life is to get closer to the pain, and the only way to do that is to feel it. So here's a rubric for remembering what to do when an emotion you don't like shows up: *feel it, don't fight it or feed it*. It teases out all the stuff that we add to the emotion that masquerades as feeling it fully or doing something worthwhile.

Fighting your emotions means trying not to have them (i.e., avoiding them), whether through your actions (drinking, working excessively, surfing social media) or through thinking. There are lots of ways we can try to think our way out of feelings—rationalizing, convincing ourselves the emotion is not justified, imagining ways of escape (winning the lottery, quitting our jobs), criticizing ourselves for what we feel, mentally rehearsing arguments, repeatedly going over the situation that evoked the feeling. The list is endless. Do you employ any of these strategies?

Feeding your emotions means giving them more power than they need. Stoking their fires. Offering them treats to snack on. This is another kind of avoidance, because it takes you away from simply experiencing the emotion as it is. Instead, you inflate it into something else. This can also take many forms. For example, if you're feeling angry, feeding your anger might look like reminding yourself over and over how you've been done wrong, imagining the evil motivation of the person who made you angry, remembering other injustices you've experienced in your life, screaming and yelling, or storming around the house. (By the way, research shows that expressing your anger in these ways usually just makes you more angry.)

So how do you *just* feel your emotions? Here's a method that can be quite useful.

Observe and Describe

Observing and describing requires some awareness of what's going on inside you, so if you want to bone up on that, review Microskills 1–3. But you can start here if you like. Here's how to do it:

1. Wait until you are feeling something that catches your attention—a flicker of sadness, a spark of joy, a swell of anxiety. Start by slowing down and taking three deep breaths.

2. Next, in your mind's eye, slowly scan your body from head to toe, observing all the places where the physical sensations that are part of your emotion manifest in your body. Remember from Microskill 4 that all emotions—anger, sadness, shame, happiness—are made up of thoughts, physical sensations, and urges.

3. As you scan, notice what the sensations are like without adding any words to them. Notice where they reside, notice where they begin and end, notice if they seem heavy or light. Hold what you notice in your awareness without judgment, without trying to fix anything.

4. The next step is to describe. Silently to yourself—or in your notebook—label what you experience with just a few simple

words. You might say something like, *I'm noticing a heaviness in my chest and a sinking feeling in my stomach.* Or *My cheeks feel hot, and I feel an urge to run away.* Try not to add a story to what you're describing. If you find yourself saying something like, *I'm noticing a heaviness in my chest because my boss is a jerk, and he doesn't pay attention me*, back off a bit, and stick to simple labels. It helps if you precede what you say with something like "I'm noticing" or "I feel."

You can stop here, or you can add one more step.

5. Give the emotion a name. See if there is an obvious name for this emotion. Is it anger? Irritability? Anxiety? Sadness? Guilt? Shame? Excitement? Joy? Or maybe a combination of these? Don't worry so much about getting it right. Identifying emotions is a skill you can build over time if you don't already have it.

This practice is designed to allow you to feel your emotions without fighting or feeding them, which are just different ways of avoiding experiencing them as they are. This will help you move toward the scary parts of life, doing what it takes to live meaningfully—even when it hurts.

Practice Willingness

Few of us *want* to have the painful internal stuff (thoughts and feelings) and external stuff (lousy circumstances) that come along with life. So we try to control that stuff by avoiding it. Remember, avoidance is just another way of controlling: if you stay away from something you don't like, you don't need to have it.

So what happens when we allow discomfort and let it be, without trying to change it? Roadblocks are a part of life, and painful thoughts and feelings are bound to arise. So let's revisit control and get to know its alternative: willingness.

The Problem of Control

Maybe you're a secret control freak like me (Matt). Well, sort of. The first time I went to therapy, I was twenty-one and pretty depressed. My girlfriend had told me she wanted to try dating other people to see what it was like. I fell apart. What made this especially complicated was that it had been my idea to start with. A few weeks earlier I had suggested we consider dating other people sometime in the future, because we were probably going to get married, and we had never dated anyone else.

I just wasn't ready to actually go through with it yet. I became pretty obsessive—not in a creepy, "I want to know what you are doing at all times" way, but in an "I can't stop thinking about you with another guy" kind of way. I lost sleep, I lost my appetite, and I lost all pleasure in life.

What I didn't know was that I was being really controlling in ways I couldn't see. My therapist, Dave, suggested that I had a problem with control. I had no idea what he was talking about—it's not like I was telling my girlfriend not to date other guys. What he meant was that I had the same problem with control that all humans have.

He speculated that I was angry but wasn't allowing myself to feel that anger. I was trying to control it by avoiding it. I didn't think I was angry. How could I be angry? Dating other people was *my idea*. Anger didn't make sense.

He observed that our emotions don't always make complete, rational sense. That's just part of being human. Our minds might have an idea about what we should feel, but often that's not what we feel. He noticed that I was weirdly reasonable about my girl-friend dating other people, despite how miserable I was. He suspected, rightly, that reasonableness was a way to stay away from anger.

We did some exploring, and it turned out he was right. I was trying desperately to control my anger, because I was worried that if I acknowledged it, I would explode, and I wouldn't be a nice guy anymore. But squashing my anger was making me miserable.

When I say "control," I mean it in the same way that you can control the presence of light in a room by flipping a light switch.

There's no emotional analog to flipping a light switch outside of taking a massive dose of drugs—and, um, that's a terrible idea.

What You Can and Can't Control

It's not that control never works. It just works less effectively and reliably than we think it does. Let's tease out exactly what we can and can't control to get a better sense of the big picture. Take a look and see if this brief—and admittedly incomplete— list rings true:

What we can't control:

- thoughts that spontaneously arise

- emotions that spontaneously arise

- spontaneous physical sensations, urges, and memories

- the thoughts and feelings of others

- what other people do and say

- our immediate circumstances

- our pasts

- our futures

What we can control:

- how we respond to our thoughts (e.g., noticing them, arguing with them)

- how we respond to our emotions (allowing them, pushing them away)

- how we respond to sensations, urges, and memories (reminding ourselves they are normal, criticizing ourselves)

- how we respond to our circumstances (problem solving, appreciating)

- how we act toward other people (kind, dismissive)

- what we choose to make important in our lives (family, work, play)

Notice that what we can't control is our immediate thoughts and feelings, the past and future, and what other people do, say, think, and feel. What we can control is how we respond to these things.

For example, if you feel anxious and eager to avoid something difficult—like being honest with your family about your sexual orientation—you can criticize yourself or offer yourself kind words. But you can't prevent that anxious feeling from arising.

If you fail something important, like a job interview or an exam, you can avoid job interviews and exams, or you can double down and face that fear of failing. But you can't make past failures go away.

And if your partner is mad at you for being insensitive, and you feel guilty, you can start an argument to avoid thinking about what you did, or you can get curious and gently ask what you could do differently in the future. But you can't erase your partner's anger.

Willingness Is the Alternative

Willingness means being open to whatever shows up. It's the opposite of control and avoidance. It also means taking actions that we know will evoke discomfort—like getting that blood test you've been avoiding, having an open conversation with your partner, or starting a new career trajectory—if doing so moves you in the direction of what you care about.

Willingness doesn't mean liking or wanting what shows up. And it doesn't mean giving up or resigning yourself to shady circumstances. It just means allowing what can't be changed in this moment to just *be*—while you focus on what can be changed.

When I agreed that I was avoiding my anger, my therapist taught me to let go of trying to control it. I learned to practice being willing to have what was already there (my anger, sadness, and guilt, as well as the fact that my girlfriend wanted to see other people) by leaning in, rather than avoiding. This new willingness made an enormous difference. I quit being so "nice" and got a lot more real. But I didn't explode, and I didn't become a jerk. Paradoxically, I quit feeling so out of control of my life and my emotions. And I stopped feeling depressed. (Later we broke up, but that's another story.)

Practicing Willingness

The next time you find yourself in a control-and-avoidance struggle, ask yourself what you can and can't control *right now*.

1. Review the list we offered and write them down in two columns in your notebook.

2. Notice the items on the "can't control" list. Ask yourself these questions: *Can I be willing to have what I have right now without trying to push it away? Can I allow what's already here to just be, rather than fighting it?*

3. Ask yourself what you would be doing in this situation if you weren't working so hard to control. If you were being your best self, living as the person you truly want to be, what might you do? Then do that—even if it's hard, even if you feel pulled toward control and avoidance.

Breathe In and Out of Pain

Pain is hard. It doesn't matter if it's physical pain, emotional pain, discomfort, sadness, or despair. Pain might be tough, but there are things you can do to face it, courageously stop avoiding it, and be present to the things you care about even when pain is there.

The Difference Between Perception and Response

One way to think about this is how we would think about physical pain. If you put your hand on a hot stove, nerve endings and pain receptors in your hand send messages to your brain. This allows you to "know" what is happening and allows activation of the muscles needed to move your hand.

Notice that the two parts of the pain are tough to separate—you touch the stove and immediately move your hand. It feels like one experience. But on the inside, you have one part of your nervous system that handles the perception of the pain and one part that handles the response to it. Pain perception and pain response.

For psychological pain, there is a similar dual pathway operating. There is the fear, sadness, hurt, discomfort, embarrassment, or other "negative" feelings and then a separate response to them. Just like physical pain, we often don't notice that these are separate. How we respond to our psychological pain greatly influences its duration and intensity. There are multiple reasons why focusing on the response to your pain can be helpful.

Showing Up for Your Pain Makes It Normal Size

Whether your pain is physical or emotional, pausing to notice what is going on is useful. Paying close attention may increase or decrease the pain in the short term, but it allows you to take full stock of what the sensation is, and especially where it is located in your body.

When you stop to take stock of your pain, you may realize that there is a tensing up that you weren't aware of before. Try it right now: check your body for any pain or tension sensations. You may notice that around a sore neck or back muscle there is a subtle "protection" offered by the surrounding muscles. If you stop and notice this, breathe, bring in some softness, and relax anything you're holding there, it often changes the original sensation and you may feel calmer about the sensation.

Working with cancer patients, I (Jen) have often marveled at the strong effect noticing, softening, relaxing, and breathing into the areas surrounding physical pain can be for some patients. It doesn't completely remove the pain, but breathing softness and relaxation into the sensation often allows us to relax just enough for the pain to be its actual size, rather than extra-bonus-sized because of all the stress we've surrounded it with. The same goes for emotional pain.

Noticing Pain Helps You Live Courageously

In addition to sometimes reducing the intensity, there is another reason to stop and notice your response to your pain: it allows you to live more flexibly with it.

Just like with the muscles in your shoulder or back, we often build a little "protection" around our hurt, sadness, fear, and grief to protect ourselves from having to feel it. For instance, when you feel vulnerable in a relationship, one way you might "tense your muscles" to overprotect yourself might be to try to control random things or avoid sharing your feelings with your partner.

When we notice this response and let emotions be their proper size, we have some options. We can let go of control, talk about what's going, or ask for the help we need. It might not go perfectly, and if it doesn't, we'll be able to handle that (normal-sized) feeling too.

Willing, Not Wanting

Showing up for our pain means stopping and facing our pain for what it actually is. That's great, but what if you don't really want to do that?

Of course you don't.

Remember that facing our pain doesn't mean liking it or wanting it or approving of it. It just means being willing to intentionally turn toward it, rather than away from it. You don't have to want the pain or tension in your back or shoulders to be able to stop, breathe, notice it, let go of anything extra you're holding around it. It just requires willingness. (For more on willingness, see Microskill 6.)

The payoff of willingness is that we can recall our intentions for our life. These are what we forget about when we're busy avoiding pain. Facing pain allows us to live courageously in the areas most important to us (see Microskill 12 for a discussion of values). This works the opposite way too—when we're in pain, physical or emotional, we tend to become so fixated on the pain and trying to control it that we forget all about who we want to be. If we take a breath, soften what we can soften, and face the pain that is there, we have the freedom to look at our intentions again. Like magic.

Breathe In and Out of Emotion

The next time an emotion grabs you (or the next time you notice an emotion while meditating), take a second to practice this small skill:

1. See if you can recognize which emotion it is and what it's called. Is it "sadness" or "pain" or "hurt" or "fear"? If you can't name it, does it feel familiar?

2. Notice where it shows up in your body. What are the sensations that accompany it?

3. Imagine breathing in and out of the physical place where you feel this emotion. That is, imagine that the air flows in and out of the space in your body that the emotion inhabits, not just your lungs. Breathe in—air filling up the emotional space in your body. Breathe out—air leaving the sensation that accompanies the pain in your body.

4. See if you can tease apart the emotion from your response to it. Are you upset about it? Scared of it? Wishing it was gone? Judging it? Try to let go of any extra-size reaction.

5. As you continue to breathe in and out of the emotion, see if you are able to allow it to be there, even if you don't particularly want it. See if you can allow it to move through you without resistance, without holding on to it or arguing with it.

PART THREE

Free Yourself from the Tyranny of Fearful Thoughts

Just like a fish swims in the ocean without realizing it is surrounded by water, we live every day inside the sea of thoughts that our mind produces. We don't actually realize that those are thoughts, because, just like the water to a fish, our sea of thoughts isn't even detectable to us. In part 3, we will focus on the ways to notice the outright lying, manipulating, and all-encompassing tyranny of our thought processes in order to overcome our fears and the avoidance this thinking produces.

We will develop this exact skill in Microskill 8: the ability to notice the *process* of thinking rather than the *content* of the thoughts. Thinking about thinking isn't something we often do—we are so busy reacting to our thoughts and believing them as true that the skill of backing up from them is one that takes some practice.

In Microskill 9, we will drill down into this idea to explore the many ways our minds try to convince us that we "know" something. This belief that we know something as truth with a capital *T* causes us to avoid things all over our lives. We will untangle this tendency and practice noticing when we actually—gasp—don't know.

Then, in Microskill 10, we introduce you to the idea of workability and the advantages of focusing on workability over truth. Looking at workability helps us shift from just automatically believing our thoughts (and reacting from them) to determining what works best in the situation.

One important way that an emphasis on workability might help us avoid less is the concept of right and wrong, which we address in Microskill 11. The urge to be right can be an overwhelmingly compelling desire, but it strengthens avoidance of thoughts and feelings and makes our lives smaller. We need a new skill to preserve our relationships and well-being.

Step Back and Notice Your Thinking

You are not your thoughts. Wait… *what?* Your mind spits out words, sentences, stories, images, memories, commentary, judgments, and predictions all day long, and this stuff captures most of your attention. So it can easily feel like this is the sum of who you are. But what your mind says is not the whole story. Try this experiment. (No, really, try it right now.)

Close your eyes and listen to the sounds around you for about thirty seconds. Afterward, open your eyes and read the next sentence. (Don't peek!)

Notice the difference between the sounds you are hearing and you, the one who is doing the listening.

Got it? There's you, and then there's the sounds—two separate things. (If you're thinking this is similar to the skill of "observing the observer" that we described in Microskill 2, you are correct. It's the same idea, with a twist.)

Next, slowly take in all the shapes, colors, and textures in your visual field. See if you can observe them as if for the first time—see things you may not have noticed before, even if you are in a familiar setting. Do this for about thirty seconds. Afterward, look down and read the next sentence.

Notice the difference between what you are seeing, and you, the person who is doing the seeing.

See what we're doing here? There's you, and there's what you see—two separate things. Obvious, right? Okay, here's where it gets a little more interesting.

Turn your attention to the sensations in your body where it makes contact with whatever you're sitting on. Notice the feelings of touch or pressure where your legs and back make contact with the surfaces they are resting against. Now notice the feeling of your feet inside your socks or shoes. Continue doing this for the next thirty seconds or so. Afterward, read the next sentence.

Notice the difference between the sensations you are feeling and you, the one who is doing the feeling. There's you, and then there's what you're feeling—two separate things.

If this seems a little counterintuitive, stay with us—it'll be worth it.

Close your eyes for about thirty seconds and just watch what shows up in your mind. If it helps, imagine you're sitting in a movie theater and watching your thoughts on the screen in front of you. If you notice yourself getting pulled into the thoughts, step back again and just watch. Afterward, open your eyes and read the next sentence.

Notice the difference between your thoughts and you, the one who is watching them. There's you, and then there's what you're watching—two separate things.

What's Going On Here?

Sure, it's easy to see a difference between you and what you hear and see. These are clearly separate things, right? But what about thoughts and feelings? A caveat: "You are not your thoughts" is not a scientific claim. "What is the self?" and different versions of "Who am I?" are questions that will continue to entertain academic and armchair philosophers for millennia to come.

What we're offering is a very useful perspective, one in which you can look at your thoughts (and everything else you experience inside you) as if you would look at something across the room. From this perspective, you are not your thoughts. They are simply experiences you have. They are a part of you, but not the sum of you. And having this perspective gives you a whole lot of freedom to do new things.

A New Kind of Freedom

Think of an old, painful thought that tends to show up for you, something like *I can't trust anyone, People will just let me down, I'll never be good enough,* or *I'm different from other people.* What if you could watch that thought when it shows up, simply notice it the way you might watch a car going by on the street?

And what if you took the perspective that that thought was not you, but rather was something you experience—something that shows up but is not any different, at its core, than a thought like *Maybe I'll have a cheese sandwich for lunch*. Whatever thoughts are made of, this old painful thought is made of the same stuff. It just happens to be a painful version of *Maybe I'll have a cheese sandwich for lunch*.

If you can "watch" your thoughts and take the perspective that you are not your thoughts, so many things become possible. You can have a thought and …

… not listen to it,

… do the opposite of what it implies, or

… notice it for what it is: a habitual behavior of your mind.

TRY THIS: think the thought, *I cannot lift my arms up above my head*, and while you do this, actually lift your arms up above your head. Now try this: think the thought, *I cannot stand on one leg*, and while you think this (and if you are physically capable), stand on one leg. Notice that the connection between thinking and doing is illusory. We can easily think one thing and do another.

That means you could think *I think I'll just bail on this party* and still go to the party. You can think *I can't trust anyone* and then take the next small step toward trusting someone you love. Your mind is not in charge. You are!

Getting Distance from Your Thoughts

Set a timer or something else that will catch your attention throughout the day. When the timer goes off, pause a moment and notice what you have been thinking.

1. As you do this, imagine yourself watching the thoughts as if from a distance. It sometimes helps to imagine them being written on the wall across the room from you or in the clouds in the sky above you. Or you could write them down on a piece of paper to cultivate a little distance between yourself and the words. Don't try to change them; don't try to make them go away. Just watch them. Notice the difference (and distance) between yourself and the thought. Remind yourself that you are not the thought. Then go back to whatever you're doing.

2. Then, when you find yourself having a difficult moment— especially when you have the urge to avoid—do the same thing: pause a moment and notice what you're thinking.

Imagine yourself watching the thoughts as if from a distance. Notice the difference (and distance) between yourself and the thought. Remind yourself that you are not the thought. It is just something you experience, and it doesn't have to be in control. *Then do the next thing you would do if the thought wasn't running your life, but instead you were following what is deeply important to you.*

This takes practice. So don't give up if it turns out to be kind of tricky. It might help if you start by noticing the difference between yourself and sounds, yourself and sights, and *then* yourself and thoughts, just as we did in this chapter. As you move forward toward reducing avoidance, facing your fears, and building a meaningful life, this skill is going to come in handy.

Admit the Truth ("I Don't Know")

Have you ever noticed the amount of crap that your mind gives you every day? It is dizzying. It is constantly evaluating, judging, criticizing—both you and everybody around you—all the time.

This phenomenon is not a malfunction. This is exactly what our minds are supposed to do to keep us safe. It was passed down through hundreds of thousands of years by our ancestors, in a way, because those who were not on the lookout didn't stick around long enough to pass on their genes.

The Problem with Mental Blathering

To counteract the effects of this "mind chatter," let's first look at why we are so prone to listening to it.

- We're used to it. Our minds give us unhelpful judgments, evaluations, and criticisms all the time.

- For some reason, we automatically think these are true, even when they're clearly not so: *If I ask for a raise, I might get fired on the spot, so I should just avoid asking altogether.*

- We believe not only thoughts about ourselves but also thoughts about other people: *Everybody else seems to have the perfect relationship. If I take a risk and ask this person out, and they say no, it will just confirm that I will be alone forever.*

- We also tend to believe all our thoughts about the motivations of other people: *She passed my work off as her own because she is such a terrible person.* This is the tendency—demonstrated by people everywhere—to see somebody do something we think they shouldn't do, and to automatically assume that they did it because they are a bad person, rather than because of factors related to the situation.

- These beliefs are often vastly different from the motivations we attribute to ourselves: *I took the last piece of pie because I am a giving person and didn't want anybody else to have to suffer the calories. So generous.* This self-serving bias causes us to attribute our own crappy behavior much more to situational factors than internal factors.

All of these ways of thinking about the world quickly become habits for us—we fall in to thinking like this without even noticing it, and we think them over and over again until they feel as true as things we detect with our five senses.

Don't Believe Everything You Think

That constancy of this string of "helpful" comments doesn't mean that the best strategy is to sit around and listen to them. In fact, going down the rabbit hole of listening to your mind is not a quick way to a rich, interesting life

Sadly, the solution to this problem is not to never let our minds judge, evaluate, and criticize. This would require either a lobotomy or a seriously big tranquilizer gun. Because, as we said, this is just something our minds do. Instead, the solution is to learn how to look flexibly at our thinking. Here's the breakdown:

- Increase your awareness that you even are thinking. This is super hard to do if you are living on auto-pilot, but if you set an intention to check in more often to see what you are thinking (see Microskills 1–3 on mindfulness or Microskill 8 on noticing your thoughts), it becomes easier and easier to catch your thoughts in flight.

- Notice that having these thoughts (even the judgy, critical ones) are your mind's job, and no thought is "good" or "bad"—they're just thoughts. We'll say that again: they're just thoughts. There are no thoughts, no matter how important, that are more than just thoughts, right? Even the thought that it would be bad if aliens blew up the planet is just a thought. Because even if we really would not like aliens to blow up the planet, all that has happened today is that you had a thought about it.

- Catch any habits your mind has. What are the go-to topics your mind jumps at? Watch for ones that say you can't handle something (just a thought), that people wouldn't love you if they knew something about you (just a thought), that this is the best book you've ever read (just a "true" thought, we concur).

- Try to generate multiple stories about the same thing. If someone is snippy with you, as soon as you decide that it's because they're an asshat, try to come up with multiple other "reasons" why they did that. We love our stories so much that we hold on to them with both hands. A good way to let go of them and think more flexibly is to write multiple stories about every situation.

Take, for instance, a situation in which you are passed up for a promotion. Maybe you think it happened because your boss doesn't like you and has it in for you. Other stories might be the following: there's another role your boss is thinking of for you; your boss is not paying attention to your awesome work; your boss is an alien disguised as a human; your boss passed you over because you wear too much plaid.

The goal here, remember, is not to change a "negative" thought into a "positive" thought. Doing so will just make "negative" thoughts something to avoid and "positive" thoughts something to grasp on to, rather than just flexibly noticing these are just thoughts (see Microskill 8 on noticing your thoughts).

TEENY TINY PRACTICE
I Don't Know

Add "I don't know" to the end of every thought for the next five minutes and see what happens. For example, if you have the thought, *This day sucks*, you can change it to *This day sucks—I don't know*. From *That person totally blew me off* to *That person totally blew me off—I don't know*. Even something like, *The sky is blue* becomes *The sky is blue—I don't know*.

This "not-knowing" isn't confusion, and it isn't doubt—it's just letting go of the idea that you (need to) know what your mind tells you that you know. See what happens.

Emphasize Workability
over Truth

If you can think about the *workability* of a thought rather than its truth, it becomes easier to stop avoiding the thought, stop being ruled by fears, and start living fully. When a thought shows up, especially one that is painful, we tend to focus on whether it is true or false. If your mind gives you *This is going to be a horrible day* or *I'm falling short as a human being,* and you want to get away from the discomfort the thought evokes, you might search for evidence that it's false or try to talk yourself into a more positive view.

But your mind is clever. It can easily come up with a fancy argument *for* just about any thought. And thinking positive thoughts to replace negative thoughts can backfire. Your mind is probably too clever and too tenacious to simply respond, *Right, I can't believe I didn't think of that before—it's clear I'm not falling short as a human being. I'm a wonderful person.*

What if, instead of focusing on truth, you focused on workability? What if you asked yourself if the thought was workable or not? "Workable" is a weird word. It's a therapist word, not a normal-person word. What it means here is "leads you toward a rich, full life." So a thought is "workable" if following where it leads moves you forward in your life, rather than backward.

Sometimes it makes more sense if you think about the opposite. "Unworkable" thoughts are thoughts that lead us—usually in order to manage our fears and internal experiences—away from who we want to be. They are *unworkable* in the long term, even if you sometimes feel better in the short term. If you are upset or frustrated with someone you love, saying something biting and cruel about them might work well to reduce your frustration in the moment or get them to do what you want them to do immediately. But it just doesn't move you toward, say, being a caring, compassionate partner.

Notice that workability isn't just about thoughts. It's also about all of our actions and reactions. What you do can be workable or unworkable. Even what you feel can be workable or unworkable. Whatever shows up inside of you, whatever urge you have, you can consider whether it's workable or unworkable to do, if it's an action, or to follow where it leads, if it's an internal experience like a thought, feeling, or urge.

Workability in Action

Let's say your partner comes home from a bad day at work and is grumpy with you—and is clearly in the wrong. You might have these kinds of thoughts: *They are being a jerk. I shouldn't have to put up with this. I don't want to be disrespected like this for the rest of my life. The only way to prevent that completely is to leave the relationship right now.*

Now these thoughts all might be 100 percent true. However, depending on what qualities you most want to have as a partner (see Microskill 12 on values), focusing on the truthfulness of these thoughts might not work as well as focusing on their usefulness. Are they useful in helping you move toward having a rich, full life? Maybe yes, maybe no.

Workable in this context might be taking a breath and letting your feelings settle before reacting. It might be that leaving the relationship is the best option for a vital life. Or it might be getting curious about what's going on behind your partner's behavior. It might be saying something kind in response or asking your partner respectfully to take a chill pill and come back when they can be nicer.

So workability is about whether something you think, feel, or do is useful or not in the long term. Does it move you toward an awesome version of yourself?

Acting with Workability in Mind

It turns out that, of the thousands of thoughts we have a day, many of them are not useful in our lives. And sometimes, that leads us to some bad shit. Take Sue, for example, who gets stressed out meeting new people. One day she meets Joe, and she has the thought *I can already tell he doesn't like me*. And who knows, maybe she's right—maybe Joe doesn't initially like her.

But think about how Sue will *act* with Joe if she is focused on whether this thought is true. Maybe she provides short answers to his first questions, maybe she asks none of her own. Maybe she gets away from him as fast as she can. According to research (Curtis & Miller, 1986), the more she focuses on his not liking her as "true," the more likely she is to act in a way that makes Joe—you guessed it—not like her.

So what might she do instead? Instead of trying to get herself to change the thought that Joe doesn't like her, she could instead focus on whether that thought and its implications are useful. Is this thought the right tool for this situation? Or is it just one of the tens of thousands she will have that day? Adding extra weight to it is something she can choose to do—or not.

The advantage to this is it allows her to focus instead on her actions. What would be a workable action for her to take in the moment when she meets Joe and thinks he doesn't like her? Well, if she values being kind and connected and building relationships, she could answer his questions thoughtfully and show curiosity about him. Even if she thought he didn't like her.

Imagine how different our lives would be if we could focus on the workability of our thoughts, urges, and actions throughout the day. Instead of walking around protecting ourselves and being reactive all the time, we would follow our intentions and move toward who we want to be instead. We could face our fears, stop avoiding our stuff, and move toward things instead of away from them.

Workability Meter

Keep your notebook by your bed. For one week, before you go to sleep each night, write down a few of the biggest things that happened that day and then write down thoughts, feelings, and urges you had in response to them and the actions you took. Then rate, on a scale of 1 to 10, how workable or useful those were. Remember, workability is about how useful they are for building a rich, full life.

Let Go of Being Right

Our minds can be real dictators sometimes. They give us a steady stream of thoughts—many about our alleged deficits, weaknesses, and failings—and they get us to act as though they are *real*, and in so doing, get us hooked on trying to fix them. Sigh.

Yes, your mind tries really hard to be ahead of the game at all times by focusing on every single flaw you (possibly) have, every mistake you (might) make, every (potentially) bad decision. And it amplifies them, just to make sure it has your full attention. Right? It likely isn't kind, and it doesn't try to be gentle in its feedback. It's not like, *Hey sweetie, that was a great effort there, but you might just consider working on X.* It's more like *What's wrong with you? You dumbass!* Something like that. Gets tiring, doesn't it?

Being Right Feels So … Right

But you know what your mind really digs? Being right. Because when you are right, somehow you are okay in the world. You are a valid human. You matter. When you speak, people should listen. Because you're right, right?

It feels good to win an argument with that contentious relative who disagrees with your politics; to outmatch that guy on the internet who thinks he knows everything; to say, "I told you so" when your partner disagrees with your directions, turns right, and gets you hopelessly lost. It's even better when they say, "Honey, you were right." Sooo satisfying. You've won. It's better than chocolate. Being right just feels so … *right*. Especially with your most strongly held beliefs.

The Backfire Effect

Interesting fact about your mind: when you are presented with evidence counter to your most strongly held beliefs, you are likely to dig in deeper rather than reconsider your position. This is called the *Backfire Effect* (Nyhan and Reifler, 2010). But why does this happen? It may be because our brain treats information that is inconsistent with our beliefs as a threat. In an fMRI study on how we process information contrasting with our most strongly held partisan political beliefs, researchers found that our brains process that information in the same way and in the same place (our cingulate cortex) that we process our response to pain (Westen et al., 2006). Simply put, our minds treat ideas we think are wrong like they are as dangerous as being physically hurt. No wonder we get so attached to being right!

Recently, I (Lisa) was walking our dogs up the hill to our house, and saw the garbage truck pick up our neighbor's garbage, but not ours. I was pissed! I ran up that hill, immediately got on the phone, called the company, asked to speak to the manager. I gave her a piece of my mind, and demanded that she call the truck and send it back to pick up the trash, dammit. The sanctimony was glorious. I was completely justified in my anger. I went on and on. I was *right*.

She called back a few minutes later, and this is how the conversation went:

Manager: What color was the truck?

Me: It was blue.

Manager: So ... our trucks are white.

Me: Oh....

Manager: Next time, before you get all mean, maybe you should make sure that you have the right truck. Our trucks haven't been to your neighborhood yet. Sweetie.

Me: ....

I wasn't right. Not even close. But in the moment, I thought I was. And it felt so good! Until it evaporated into embarrassment and shame.

The High Cost of Being Right

Attachment to being right all the time comes at a cost. Sure, you might win. But what is it you win? Let's take a deep dive into this: even if you win, it might be important to consider what you lose when you win the "I'm the rightest" competition. Think about how winning this competition might impact the people around you whom you care about, who wish to be heard by you, and who wish to be close and connected with you.

TRY THIS: Take a few moments to call to mind a situation in which you needed to be right, at all costs. Once you have it, slow yourself down, and imagine the scene as though you are an observer—a fly on the wall. Imagine observing yourself in the scene as you were then, attached to being right, to winning. Notice how you are behaving; notice how that is landing on those around you. Whom are you with? How are they feeling? What are you noticing as you observe yourself, acting as you did then? Do you like this person that you were then? How connected did you feel to those people you care about? Did your efforts to make yourself *right*—and to make them *wrong*—bring you closer to them? Or further away?

Perhaps you won the campaign to be right. Perhaps that was enough. But usually, this comes at the cost of connection to those you care most about.

When Do We Most Need to be Right?

It might be useful to give some thought to those things that we find uber-important to be right about. Consider the following:

- You feel wronged by someone—and feel you need them to recognize that and atone.

- You feel like you have a great, unrecognized talent—and harbor resentment about others who are noticed and applauded, while you are not.

- You feel that you know how to parent—but your partner disagrees, and this leads to arguments in bed every night, and you both fall asleep angry.

For everyone it might be something different. At the core, however, it works pretty much the same way. Being right is a façade you wear so you don't feel vulnerable. And you are most likely to put it on when you are *feeling* most vulnerable. Remember, your mind views being wrong as physical danger. So being right can be a way to avoid feeling vulnerable.

Beginner's Mind

There's a Buddhist saying: In the mind of a beginner, there are many possibilities. In the mind of an expert, there are few. It boils down to this: if you are attached to being right, you are unteachable; you cannot learn or change or evolve. What if you had to choose between being right all the time, and

... being really connected to those people you love?

... real intimacy with the people most important to you?

... truly learning, so you can adapt and handle stuff with flexibility and grace?

What would you choose? What *do* you choose, most frequently, in your life right now?

Be willing to take off your armor, to lay down your arms, as this could be the key to discovering who you are, all that you are capable of, and the things that truly matter to you. Want to find out?

Choosing Vulnerability

Try this on for size. Call it a vulnerability practice. There are only three steps:

1. If you find yourself in a situation in which you need to be right, pause.

2. While you are pausing, slow down, and notice your intention. What's your behavior about? What kind of vulnerability are you trying to stay away from? Hurt? Disappointment? Disappointing somebody else? Being wrong? Feeling scared? Having made a mistake? Feeling sad?

3. If you pause and notice what vulnerability you're avoiding in this moment, this opens up the possibility of choosing to keep your intention or maybe to allow yourself to show up— as you are—and risk being seen for who you are.

Experiment with this. Sometimes, stick with being right. See how that works for you. Then switch it up—instead of working on being right, choose another intention that will help you build greater intimacy and connection in your life. For example, you could choose between working on being right and

- being kind;

- being connected;

- gaining intimacy;

- learning from those around you;

- trying on the perspective of someone else;

- letting go of control;

- allowing yourself to surf that feeling of uncertainty, of possibility; or

- letting yourself be vulnerable.

We can't tell you what will happen next. That's for you to find out!

PART FOUR

Shift Your View So It's Bigger Than Your Fears

When your focus is on your feelings and trying to control them, avoidance is the response that just makes sense. The goal of this section is to widen your focus from the things you're trying to avoid inside your skin to the ways you want to be in the world.

We come into each day with an opportunity to live our best life. However, most of the time we aren't thinking about how we want to be in our lives or our intentions for the day. In this section of the book, we will help you develop skills that will broaden your view so that you focus more on your intentions and less on your fears.

Starting with Microskill 12, you clarify your values—what is most important to you. This allows you to create a roadmap of your intentions and a broader sense of what is meaningful in your life. Everybody has different values, and different values may be more important at different times in your life; identifying how you want to be now is the first step.

Next you will take those abstract values and turn them into specific actions that will enrich your life. Sometimes when we clarify our values, it can be a little overwhelming to think about how to incorporate them into our day-to-day experience, especially when avoiding our feelings has been our biggest concern. Microskill 13 focuses on the empowering practice of engaging in actions that support your values.

To make this process even more concrete, Microskill 14 helps you pick one specific thing to do. Since habitual behavior often works toward the goal of avoidance, we want to pick specific steps to start living values. This practice will help you create a life you are proud of, one step at a time.

Human beings have an enormous capacity to take different perspectives about ourselves, others, our future selves—you name it. This ability to take and change perspectives allows us to shift how we see our experiences. Microskill 15 develops the ability to flexibly change perspective to give you more freedom to take actions toward your values, even when you're really anxious or sad.

One thing that can help change our focus from avoiding our fears is to take a look at the role of identity plays in our actions. When you feel that your identity is on the line, it's difficult not to put all of your energy and attention onto avoiding negative feelings. Microskill 16 can loosen your hold on the idea of "self" to allow for a more flexible way of responding to difficult thoughts and feelings.

The last skill in this section targets boldness. A focus on avoiding our experiences necessarily creates a smaller life. Microskill 17 develops the ability to take bold steps toward what is most meaningful and to expand your life by focusing on meaning and purpose.

Author Your Values

Who do you most want to be in this life? It's such a big question that we rarely bother to ask it of ourselves. When we think about our values, we tend to think of them as things we inherited from our parents or ways of being that we acquired over the course of our lives.

Let's take a more active perspective. What if we think about values as something that we can choose on purpose as a guide for our future behavior? What would you come up with? Do you want to be funny and fun? Present and aware? Thoughtful and compassionate? Honest and direct? A little of all of these? A whole different list?

Thinking ahead of time about how we want to be in our lives is not something humans tend to do. I don't know about you, but I (Jen) tend to opt for the "react and apologize" path through life. Yet there is a way to have a clear sense of what path to take so we can feel proud of ourselves later.

Consider a recent conflict you had with somebody. Maybe a family member hurt your feelings, or a misunderstanding led to strong feelings or strong words. When you think about that situation, whose behavior are you focused on? Who would need to change to make the situation better? The answer is often: the other person. We tend to look at other people's behavior and focus on what we think could have been different. While they may be deeply and importantly wrong, the problem with focusing on them is that you don't have any control over their behavior, just your own.

How do you want to be in situations in which somebody does something obnoxious or annoying to you? *How do you want to be* in the face of difficult situations, knowing that difficult situations are always going to be there? Maybe your answer is *calm* or *patient* or *direct* or *transparent*. Maybe your answer is *compassionate, forgiving,* or *assertive*—or *understanding*. There isn't a wrong answer.

The important thing is that your focus is on your own behavior, not the other person's. Even when the other person's side of the street is so tempting to focus on, you have control over only your side of the street, so sweep it.

Do It for You

There is an important implication to this idea. It involves changing the focus of your behavior from other people (How will they respond? Will they be upset?) and onto yourself (Is this consistent with your values? Are you proud of yourself for this move?)

This is not comfortable for everybody. We are often raised to be focused on the impact or outcome of our behavior on others, rather than the impact or process of the behavior on ourselves. Here's an example, since this can be a little tricky to understand.

I (Jen) am married to a man who likes the bed made. I myself don't care at all whether the bed is made (nobody tends to see it but us, and we're just going to get right back in it and mess it up the next time we go to bed). That being said, when I think about what kind of partner I want to be, the word "thoughtful" always comes to mind. It's just a huge value of mine, and I'm always looking for ways to be a more thoughtful person, particularly with my partner.

So when I'm the last person out of the bed, I try to remember to make the bed. I want to be clear: I don't make it for my husband. I make it because at the end of the day, I want to be able to pat myself on the back and say "I was a thoughtful partner today." My vitality comes from living my values. This means that it is okay if he doesn't thank me or if he doesn't acknowledge my awesome bed-making skills. I didn't do it for him. I did it to move toward my "thoughtful partner" values.

Our vitality comes from doing things that matter to us, not from making other people happy or pleased with us. In fact, research shows that not only do we experience more vitality when we're engaged in goals that matter to us than when we are engaged in goals that matter to other people, but our vitality increases in moving toward our own goals regardless of whether we feel happier doing it (Nix et al., 1999). When we focus less on making people happy—which is temporary and not usually under our control—and more on doing things that matter to us, we will experience more vitality in our lives.

What Are Your Values?

A key part of living your values is figuring out what they are. They change over time, we prioritize them differently depending on what's going on, and different values matter to each of us. An easy way to start authoring your own values is with the broadest list possible.

So, *what are the five most important qualities you want to have in this life?* We'll get more specific later, but in general, what five adjectives would you most want to describe you? Here are some examples to pick from if you have a hard time generating them from scratch:

accepting, accountable, altruistic, ambitious, assertive, attentive, aware, balanced, bold, brave, careful, committed, communicative, compassionate, competent, connected, consistent, contributing, cooperative, courageous, creative, curious, decisive, dependable, determined, disciplined, empathic, enthusiastic, ethical, expressive, fair, family oriented, fearless, fun, generous, giving, graceful, grateful, honest, honorable, humble, imaginative, independent, innovative, inquisitive, insightful, intuitive, irreverent, kind, learning focused, loving, loyal, open, passionate, patient, persistent, playful, poised, present, productive, professional, purposeful, recreation focused, reflective, respectful, responsible, selfless, sensitive, service oriented, sincere, spiritual, spontaneous, stable, supportive, thankful, thorough, thoughtful, tolerant, transparent, trusting, trustworthy, truthful, understanding, welcoming

Do you have your list written down in your journal? Again, this doesn't have to be the list for the rest of your life, but it is useful to be able to have them handy—this is why we want you to pick only five, so you can easily tick them off on your fingers when you are unsure how to move forward or are stuck in a situation.

Values and Goals and Actions

You may notice that the list in the previous section includes just general values. There are no goals or actions in that list. That is on purpose: values are general directions, and moving toward them often involves specific actions related to specific goals (check out Microskill 13, "Make Values a Verb" and Microskill 17, "One Small, Bold Move at a Time" for more about specific valued actions).

For instance, you might want to be a connected friend (your value), which would involve making regular plans to spend time with your close friends (your goal), including asking them if they want to meet up for dinner this week (an action). Or, in the example described above, my wanting to be a thoughtful partner (value), leads to my looking for ways to do nice things for my partner (goal), and to making the bed when I'm the last one out of it (action).

While it can be useful to have your broadest values available at your fingertips, it can also sometimes be valuable to dig down a little deeper into your values in specific domains. For this practice, use your journal to list your most important values in your romantic relationships, friendships, family relationships, professional life, education, spirituality, community, and health You may not have strong values in every area, but listing values in the areas that matter will give you a great roadmap for generating goals and actions to bring more vitality into your life.

Make Values a Verb

Dream big, they say. Still, avoidance shows up in our lives when we begin to wish for things we really care about, or when we think about striving to be our best selves. When I (Lisa) was a child, I was fascinated by Mount Everest. I watched every documentary there was about mountain climbing and read all the books. I dreamed of one day going there, seeing it. Also, I was not in the least athletic. I was nearly always the last one chosen to be on the kickball team because I was small and chubby, ran slowly, and was pretty obviously uncoordinated. My mind was all over this and shut down the Everest dream years ago as utterly ridiculous.

Even so, a few years ago I trekked to Everest Base Camp with my daughter. It was one of the hardest, most physically strenuous and emotionally challenging things I've ever done—and also one of the most incredible and life-changing experiences I've ever had! How does one clumsy, sedentary person go from couch potato to seventeen thousand feet? The short answer is: one small—sometimes very small—step at a time, in the service of a really big dream that makes all the effort worth it.

Your Inner Critic Versus Your Best Self

When you think about applying for that "reach" school or dream job or starting that moonshot project, what do you notice your mind saying? Does it usher you forward, without reservation? Or, rather, does it carefully bring each and every risk and pitfall to your attention? Maybe it details character flaws that will lead you to stumble and fall short.

For many of us, this is a way we come face to face with our inner critic, whose job is to help us avoid harm—even if that avoidance prevents us from moving forward in ways that make us feel like our lives are meaningful and fulfilled. If it were up to the critic, we'd never move far off our couches—too dangerous out there in the world, you see.

Has getting hooked by your thoughts stopped you from being your best self? Take a few moments to consider the things you value, which we discussed in the previous chapter. Are there places in your life that you would like to go but haven't because your critic tells you it isn't possible or that you're not enough or that you will likely fail?

See if you can slow down and notice what turning away from important things feels like. Perhaps you notice a sense of relief. Or maybe also you catch a tinge of regret or sadness. It may be that your critic tells you that your dream of something different is just too big, too overwhelming. The critic may chime in with thoughts like, *I can't because I'm not _____ enough.*

What if your best self is, in fact, what you do? You can always, in any moment, take small steps toward being your best self and living your best life.

Living the Dream

We all have good intentions. Once you've identified your values, take some time allowing them to take up residence in your heart. That's the first step toward living them, one small move at a time. Remember, values are not goals, although you may shoot for goals in the service of your value. Values are things that inspire action—for example, you may value being a good friend, or you may value authenticity or learning or service.

TRY THIS: Take a few moments to close your eyes and connect in with your breath. Check in with your body and see how it is doing. Call to mind an image of a future you'd like to inhabit— or the type of person you'd most like to become. What do you see yourself doing? What types of qualities or characteristics do your actions reflect? In a world where it is possible to be your best self, what would that look like? Allow yourself to dream big. What are the underlying motives for this best self?

Once you've connected to your values, think about what behaviors or steps that you can do or take to move you in that direction. For example, if one of my values is to care for my body, one step I might take would be to go to the gym or eat a more plant-based diet. If appreciating the world is important to me, I might spend more time in nature. If I value ambition, I might work harder at studying or staying later at work.

As you do this, your mind may tell you how none of this is possible, that it's too much, that you can't do it—but don't get caught up in it! The bigger the step, and the more you care about taking it, the louder your mind will get. See if that isn't so! When this happens, see if you can make those steps as little as they need to be. You need only do the next right thing in this exact moment. If going to the gym feels too big, maybe choose to walk the dog instead; if you're having trouble focusing, perhaps take many brief breaks so you can focus well in shorter bursts. Once you have your small steps mapped out, make a promise to yourself, and do it. When your mind says you can't, do it anyway. Repeat.

Give yourself props for the effort, not the outcome. You are not in charge of the outcome—only of the steps. You will almost certainly fall down and swerve off the path at times. We all do. And when that happens, see if you can gently bring yourself back, one little step at a time, to the path toward your best life.

Actions that Follow Values

Each day, take a few moments to connect with the things you really care about. Perhaps these involve people that you love, or perhaps the "why" that inspires you to be your best self. Think of one small thing you can do each day that will be a small step in that direction. Say this to yourself, or if you prefer, write them down in your journal. In the blank, state the step you will take, and be specific and concrete:

- *Today, I will take this step in the service of my values: _____, even if (when) it's hard, even if I don't feel like it, and even if my mind says I can't.*

Now go do it and see where it takes you.

Change the Small Stuff

When we do the same stuff, the same way, all the time, there's no opportunity for learning or for new experiences that matter to us. This is just as true for the habit of avoiding stuff as it is for our morning routine.

Have you got a morning routine? Alarm goes off, and you hit snooze three or four times, roll out of bed, shower, get dressed, make coffee, let dogs out, get into car, and head off to work. Day in, day out. Works pretty well. Routines help keep you in your lane. They're comfortable—like an old pair of shoes. Routines let you go on autopilot. You get so used to them, you don't even need to pay attention. But there are downsides.

Crap—where did I leave my car keys? You didn't notice because your mind was spinning off elsewhere. Or there's that one extra errand you need to run, but you are completely stressed, because it doesn't fit with your routine, and it's tough to be flexible. Or maybe you didn't notice your partner looked pretty sad this morning, as you went your merry way through your routine. They needed to connect—but that got inked into the "missed opportunities" section of your day. On Tuesday, your alarm didn't go off, and you arrive to work late, flustered, and worried about what your boss will think—because there was a snafu, and your routine didn't work.

When Avoiding Tough Stuff Becomes Routine

Routines work, until they don't. And they can get so well worn that it's hard to get out of them. Is avoiding the tough stuff a routine you follow? Maybe you're on autopilot so you don't have to face your discomfort. Consider these examples:

- You want to ask that cool person you saw on your dating app out, but you're worried they'll say no, so you don't. Swiping left—or avoiding that risk— becomes routine.

- You could ask to lead that project, but you might screw up, and then everyone will know you are a poser. So you keep quiet. Taking a backseat—and staying in it—becomes your thing.

- Things aren't going great at school—classes are hard, and you're not really clicking with anyone. So you stay in bed. Pretty soon, you've chalked up more days spent in bed than in class.

Over and over and over. It starts to feel like these are the only ways for you to be and also that they *mean something about you:* that these patterns *sum up who you are.* When you follow the same routines to avoid doing hard stuff, those things that you are avoiding can feel bigger and more daunting. They can get so big that you might feel like it's impossible to face them. You might get used to the idea that how you deal with them through avoidance is the *only* thing you *can* do when they show up. So how do you flex up and venture off that well-worn, one-way street?

Doing Something Different

All it takes is two small steps, applied to more and more situations. Along the way, you'll discover the wonder of showing up for life afresh.

1. Do something different about some uncomfortable or hard thing you normally avoid—even a small thing. Walk a different way to class. Show your boss some work product and ask for feedback. Try a new kind of coffee.

2. Get curious about what might happen. Slow down, wake up, and pay attention. Wonder. Your mind will jump in with reasons why you should have stayed in your routine, because the world is somehow risky or dangerous outside of that. Simply notice that, and stick with curiosity.

Having a hard time thinking up stuff you're willing to do differently? Is your mind telling you it will be too difficult? Of course you are—and of course it is. That's what minds do. Your mind likes keeping you in your track because its job is to keep you safe—and trying new stuff, according to your mind, feels inherently less safe, less certain. So if your mind is giving you a hard time about this, here are some simple things you could do *outside* your normal routine.

- Say hi to one person you don't know today. Notice what your mind says to you when you do this. Notice what the person's response is.

- If you're stuck in traffic and doing everything you can to distract yourself from feeling frustrated, slow down, and wonder about that frustration. What if you just relaxed into it, acknowledged it, and got curious about what it was like?

- Take a risk at work or in class—raise your hand and speak up. Notice what it's like to feel uncertain about how it will go, and do it anyway.

What will happen next? Ponder that, get curious, pay attention, and just watch yourself look for the next adventure that proves you can face life to be your best self.

Take Perspective

Do you ever spend more time in other people's heads than you spend in your own? For example, when you are out and about during your day, do you find yourself worrying about what other people think and how they might perceive you? *Does she think my outfit is stupid? He's thinking I'm overbearing. OMG, this presentation is going horribly—everyone hates it.* If you are like most people, it's probably hard to get your mind to stop, well, reading *other* people's minds, because you're most likely doing it to avoid what's going on in your *own* mind.

Our perspective in life determines how we get on in the world, how we interact with others, and how we behave in our communities. To take perspective means to shift your vantage point from where it is now to somewhere else. We commonly talk about it in terms of empathizing with others: we walk in someone else's shoes so that we can help them or soothe them, strategize about what their next move might be in a chess game, or understand where they are coming from. This "shift" involves an understanding of a few key concepts: that I am different from you, that I am here and you are there, and this is now and that was then.

Learning new ways to take perspective makes many things possible. We can also take perspective on ourselves in more flexible ways—for instance, on our actions and the thoughts and feelings that make up our inner experience. This involves the awareness that you are not your thoughts: you *have* thoughts, but your thoughts alone do not sum up all of who you are. Your thoughts come and go, but you are an *observer* of these thoughts—and from that observing vantage point, you remain still while your thoughts flicker in and out of your awareness. Thus, taking perspective on your inner experience allows you to simply notice your thoughts and feelings as if from a distance, as we encourage you to do it in various places throughout this book (see Microskills 2, 4, 5, 8).

The Many Benefits of Perspective

Noticing this distinction between yourself and your thoughts and feelings may make them feel less powerful, may weaken their gravitational pull on your attention. You are so much more than anything you think or feel in any moment. Thoughts and feelings are simply experiences you have—and temporary ones at that.

Taking perspective on your own behavior can also be useful in helping you track how well your actions reflect the person you most want to be—or to become. Do your actions jive with your aspirations? Or are you talking the talk, without really walking the walk? Asking these questions can be enlightening, giving you a direction in which to grow and strive.

Essentially, taking perspective can help you notice a distinction between yourself and the roles you inhabit. Sure, you might be "an only child," "a recovering alcoholic," "an accountant," "a soccer mom," and a million other things, but none of these is you. They are simply the labels you, and perhaps others, ascribe to you. You don't have to live out what these labels might imply if you don't want to. (See Microskill 16 for some more thinking on this point.)

Empathy and Forgiveness

When you're ascribing thoughts to other people, imagining all their thoughts and perceptions about something, and you remind yourself that mindreading is actually impossible, you will be more able to compassionately let people be. Their thoughts are out of your reach—and control.

At the same time, being able to take other people's perspective and consider their point of view has a really big upside: it facilitates not only empathy, but also compassion—and forgiveness. If I can put myself in your shoes, however imperfectly, I can imagine that you are *also* not your thoughts and feelings. And you are not your roles. And you are not your actions, even the ones that might drive me crazy. And maybe what's going on for you is just as complicated as what goes on for me. And thus, I can have some understanding and patience with you. We all make mistakes; we all strive to be our best selves, and at times, we miss the mark.

Flexible Perspective Taking

During your day, make some time to notice

- that you are not your thoughts, and that your thoughts do not capture all that you are;

- what it might be like in someone else's shoes (say, someone close to you who you care a good deal about); and

- what it might be like in someone else's shoes with whom you disagree, or who you feel may have treated you wrongly.

If you find yourself stuck trying to read the thoughts of others, take some perspective on this behavior: it's just your mind, doing its thing, talking away. Notice once more that you are not your thoughts.

Be the "You" You Want to Be

Who am I? That's a question many of us ask ourselves. We can ask it at three in the morning, during a dark night of the soul, as in, *Who am I, and how did I go wrong?!* Or we can ask it during some big transition, like looking for a job: *Who am I, and what do I really want to do with my life?* Or we can ask it during some period of self-discovery, like if we go to therapy: *Who am I? I need to find myself.*

We are often encouraged to clear away the layers of the façade—all the ways in which we are subtly "false" to get along—and get down to who we really are. We're told an authentic "you" is underneath those layers, and by identifying this "you" and living it out more authentically, we can feel happier. That makes a lot of sense, right? But how do we know when we get to the real one? Is there any way to really know? No one has invented a real-o-meter to tell us we have finally discovered ourselves.

Here's another possibility: what if there is no "you" underneath it all, and, instead, the "self" is something that we create, over and over again, over time? From this perspective, it can be argued that "you" is just the story—or stories—you tell yourself about who you are.

Creating Ourselves through Stories

The writing of this story of self begins when we are very small, as our caregivers tell us who we are in relation to other people. As a baby, we hear people say things to us like, "I'm mommy." "I'm daddy." "Who's a _____ [beautiful, strong, happy] baby? You are!"

Over the course of our lives, we learn a distinction between ourselves ("I") and other people ("you," "him," "her," "them"). Without even thinking about it, we begin to attach stories to this "I": "I'm a bad dancer," "I'm uncomfortable in social situations," "I'm an only child," "I'm a good student." This is normal. As we repeatedly talk about "I" and "you," we create narratives to chronicle what "I" and "you" are like and what they are capable of. It goes on all the time—we just don't notice it.

The Downside of Storytelling

There's nothing inherently wrong with this storytelling. In fact, it's inevitable. But it can have a downside. Stories become confining when we don't notice that they are just our best attempts to understand ourselves and communicate that understanding with others. We tend to think they capture the whole, definitive truth, which they couldn't possibly, and we live them out, staying within the lanes that they create for us. They then become self-fulfilling prophecies.

Take a story like "I'm socially awkward." Let's say you are kind of socially anxious, and socializing in groups, on average, tends to be hard for you. As a result, you tend to get sweaty and say the wrong thing at the wrong time.

What this story obscures are the times when you haven't been socially awkward. You probably didn't even notice them. Or you discounted them as an aberration rather than the norm. Also, "socially awkward" is in the eye of the beholder. You have no idea what other people are thinking. And people who are socially anxious tend to think a lot about what other people are thinking about them—much more than they are.

This kind of confining storytelling had a big impact on me (Matt) early in my life. It wasn't until I was well into college that I could easily "make the first move," so to speak, with anyone I was attracted to. Starting in junior high school, I was occasionally fortunate enough to find myself in a situation where there was the possibility of kissing the person I was with: I was attracted to her; she was attracted to me. We were alone. Neither of us had a humongous zit. There was nothing in my teeth. There was nothing in her teeth. We hadn't just gotten our braces tightened. In other words, kissing was a total possibility. Awesome!

However, despite my best intentions, I rarely kissed anybody. Whenever I found myself in a situation with some possibility of kissing, my story of myself showed up, front and center: I can't do this. I'm not that kind of guy who can make the first move.

So there were times when a girl was waiting for me to kiss her, and I was just not kissing her. I often discovered later that these girls got really mad at me. They thought, "What's wrong with me? Why won't this guy kiss me?" At summer camp one year, the morning after a night sitting awkwardly on the front porch of my cabin, definitely not kissing, the girl stormed up to me, steam coming out of her ears, and planted one right on my lips. She then walked away and never spoke to me again. I had been too busy stuck in my own story to actually be with her. And I had missed a golden opportunity for a first kiss.

There are two consequences to adhering to stories so you can avoid feeling uncomfortable. First, you miss out on all the rich, amazing stuff that comes with showing up to life. Second, the over-focus on yourself reinforces the story you're trapped in. You might only notice an exaggerated version of yourself—that you are sweating too much or stammering or jumping into the conversation awkwardly. A version of yourself that most people around you are not really even noticing.

Hold Your Stories Lightly

Let's go back to that socially awkward example. What if the socially awkward person could enter a social situation without that story being front and center? Would sweating, stammering, and clumsily getting a word into the conversation mean that much? Or would it just be a small part of the bigger picture? One way to find out would be to practice holding the story of who you are lightly.

TRY THIS: Explore for yourself by examining your own story. First, get a sense of what that story is. Let's say you have five minutes to tell a complete stranger who you are, what you are like, what your strengths and weaknesses are. What might you say? Take a moment to jot these down in your journal.

Next, consider the story you'd like to tell about who you are. In this story, are you brave? Kind? Persistent? Connected? Whatever characteristics you wish to embody, jot those down. If these sound like the values words we described in Microskills 12 and 13, that's because they are! Remember, values are ways that we choose to engage the world. And while you can't control whether you feel kind or connected, for example, you can behave in ways that are kind and connected. You always have that choice, no matter what you are feeling.

The next time you are in a situation that triggers a story of who you are, hold that narrative lightly enough to image a new one that you can create, one act at a time. Think about actions you can take that are consistent with a different story of you and give them a try. It might feel hard or weird—and it also might be awesome and inspiring and give you a lot more space in your life to grow.

When I got to college, I was talking with a friend one night, and we both realized that we were stuck in this story that we were not the kind of guys who made the first move. We were both interested in mindfulness meditation, along with the idea that our minds create our realities (dude!). So we wondered what would happen if we just decided that we were the kind of guys who made the first move. And we started doing it.

What happened? You guessed it: we became kissing machines! No, not really, but when we really liked someone, we just leaned in and went for it. And thankfully, it always worked out. A few years after college, when I was on a first date with my future wife, the moon was out, we were standing on a bridge looking over a river, and the universe was screaming, "This is the perfect time to kiss her!" And I did. I was willing to take the risk and see what happened.

TEENY TINY PRACTICE
Inhabiting a New Self

Each day, take a few moments to connect with a different story, one that tells the tale of who you want to be, and practice taking one small action that is consistent with that self. Along the way, notice when your old, worn story shows up—no need to fight it or rewrite it. Simply allow it, and don't let it dictate your next chapter! Write about it in your journal.

Make One Small, Bold Move at a Time

What does it mean to be bold? In Irish culture, "bold" children are naughty children; boldness is something that is punished. But boldness also means doing something brave, making your mark, taking a big step. It involves huge risk. It's high stakes. It can also mean trying something really different from we have done in the past. Swerving, willingly, off the beaten path in the service of discovering something new about ourselves, uncovering latent skills we never knew we had. Sometimes it's taking a first stab at something we really want to do—when we have no idea how to do it. It can mean efforts to fix a problem that feels … unfixable. Impossible. To be bold is to leap without a safety net. To leave it all on the field.

Boldness is about discovery, and that can be a scary thing. Boldness means acting outside your comfort zone. It means accepting the possibility that you may fail spectacularly, and then getting up and striving again. The magic is in the action—not in the outcome, which is always uncertain. It's full of possibility, potentiality.

What are the biggest risks you yearn to take? In relationships? In being your authentic self? In striving for something really big—at work? In school? Career changes? Saying a hard thing to someone we love? Doing something that you are not skilled at but that you really care about? That difficult conversation? Leaving a relationship? Starting a relationship? Asking for a raise? Becoming an entrepreneur?

You may avoid doing bold things because it preserves "possibility" and ensures that you never "fail." If you never try, then you can never fail. Sometimes people live their whole lives that way—wishing and not doing. We get good at making excuses, rationalizing why the plan would never work, why it's a much better idea to not do it. And yet, and yet. Your heart may have a hard time letting this go. So how do we move into bold action?

Diving into the Spin

Taking bold actions almost always means trying new things and moving into unknown territory. Consider the story of Lincoln Beachey, who was born in 1887. As a child, he was wild about flying and dreamed of becoming a pilot and taking to the sky about ten years after the Wright Brothers had their first flights. This was at a time when planes were incredibly primitive.

He couldn't get a job as a pilot, so instead, he started working as a flight mechanic at airshows. Eventually, he had a big break. In the Los Angeles airshow, one of the pilots was injured during a flight and unable to fly. The organizers needed someone to take a plane up, and Beachey offered to do it. Up he went, and once he got up to about three thousand feet, the motor of the plane suddenly stalled, causing it to drop and begin to spiral.

At the time, one in three flights ended in disaster, because no one had yet figured out how to get out of spiral. Pilots tried reasonable things, like trying to turn the plane in the opposite direction or pulling up, none of which worked. But Beachey made a bold move and did the opposite, the absolute craziest thing—he turned the plane's nose down and dove into the spin. Lo and behold, this unexpected, innovative move let him float right out of the spin and land safely. This changed the history of aviation forever and saved the lives of countless pilots. It also gave Lincoln Beachey a reputation as the greatest aviator of all time.

Embracing Uncertainty

Could you dive into the spin in your own life, right your direction, and turn toward your goals? The more improbable the outcome seems, the less willing we typically are to make a move. Thus, embracing uncertainty, even when your mind places potential heartbreak in front of you as a barrier, is a critical piece of taking bold action. Crazy as it sounds, we must let go of the outcome.

To do this, step back from your thoughts and sift through what your mind gives you. Look for what may be useful information, and what is simply your mind working hard to get you to avoid risk altogether. Some information will be useful in planning out logistics, timing, and so on, since our minds are essential problem-solving tools—always planning ahead and helping guide effective action. However, other information your mind throws at you will be superfluous—meant to swerve you off your path, back into safety and certainty, back to your comfort zone—and out of boldness and possibility. Naturally, when this happens, you'll notice your willingness to act shrinking. Ask yourself this question: *Am I willing to make a small, bold move, even if it means I will be outside of my comfort zone—even if it means I may crash and burn, in the service of my values?*

Notice that willingness is not a feeling, but a quality of action: it is saying yes—and meaning it (check out Microskills 6 and 25 for more on willingness). You can set yourself up with a team to support you in making your bold moves. One way to do this is to make a public commitment—tell a friend what you are planning to do so they can check in with you on how it went. If this doesn't fit for you, you might simply make the commitment out loud to yourself. Either way, research shows that making a public commitment to do something can support more effective action.

Making Bold Moves

As you've gone through these microskills, you've been practicing taking small steps into a life you could love and working on action that is consistent with your best self. Now, we'd like to give you an opportunity to move toward something really bold in your life. Choose an area where you may have been wanting to go, but where the risk is great and your mind is loud. Make a commitment to do one small, bold move each day that will head you in that direction. Tell a friend—that will help hold you accountable. Time to dive into the spin and set your life to land where you want to be.

PART FIVE

Take Small Steps Toward More Engagement

When we disrupt the pattern of avoidance that overwhelms our lives, we open up space to focus upon all the amazing things around us. Engaged in the struggle with anxiety or sadness or painful memories, there is no room left for noticing a beautiful sunrise or the overwhelming love you feel for someone you care about. In this section of the book, we will cultivate skills to enhance our lives and attend to all the wonderful things around us.

One tricky thing about cultivating the good is that we're so used to trying to shift our focus from "negative" experiences to "positive" experiences as a way of avoiding. Modern culture repeatedly tells us to use happiness or gratitude as a way to feel less anxiety or pain. Hopefully you've learned in earlier sections that this type of avoidance—even though it is our habitual nature—just doesn't work well for us in the long term. Trying to have more "good" emotions will get us in the same trap.

Instead, you can allow the amazing to really sink in, but from a place less concerned about controlling the difficult. Microskill 18 will develop skills for creating a new habit of systematically noticing the extraordinary things you miss every day as you focus on your story and controlling your experiences.

Next we emphasize gratitude. Gratitude and gratefulness, when used as a way to notice the good rather than control the bad, can enhance many aspects of your well-being and enrich your relationships, and Microskill 19 describes how to bring more of it into your life. Relatedly, Microskill 20 specifically targets the amazing world around us and ways to cultivate more appreciation, wonder, and awe with our lives and our natural surroundings.

Finally, you'll explore love and compassion. Microskill 21 develops skills for providing yourself with compassion grounded in awareness and a sense of kindness. Microskill 22 targets skills for developing an open heart and compassion and lovingkindness for people in your life and beyond.

MICROSKILL 18 Notice Positive Emotions Too

Happiness, happiness, happiness. We love happiness. Can't get enough of it. We are obsessed with being happy. All. The. Damn. Time. But what is the effect of seeking all of this happiness? Have you ever noticed that the harder you try to be happy, the more difficult it is?

Throughout this book, we have been focused on the simple fact that avoiding difficult thoughts and feelings tends to reduce quality of life over time. Remember that avoiding difficult experiences is a natural thing to do, we come by it honestly, and it often works in the short term. But as a long-term strategy, it tends to make our lives smaller rather than bigger.

So it can be a little confusing in a book like this to come across a chapter on positive emotions—haven't we been harping this whole time about accepting negative emotions instead of trying to change them into positive ones?

Ten Thousand Joys and Ten Thousand Sorrows

Think about this Buddhist expression: "life is full of ten thousand joys and ten thousand sorrows." Life is full of countless boulders in the road that are natural and normal, and we want to notice and experience them rather than trying to avoid them, but it is also full of countless *joys*, and we equally want to notice and experience those. The trick is to examine our expectations and biases, which can cloud our actual experience.

I (Jen) recently had a time of intense work, which was to be followed by a big, fabulous vacation. I cannot begin to describe how excited I was for this vacation, and in planning for it, I kept thinking about how absolutely ecstatic I was going to be once it finally came along. And when it arrived it was … fine. Not surprisingly, it didn't match the hype.

According to researchers (Mauss et al., 2011), I'm not alone in my Vacation Disappointment Disorder; the more we think something will produce positive emotions, the more we are actually likely to feel *unhappy* when it happens. It's like the more we think it is going to be great, the more disappointed we are when it is neutral or even good.

Negativity Bias

Another factor that can interfere with our ability to be present to the joys in our life is our negativity bias. As we talked about in Microskill 4, emotions have an evolutionary purpose, particularly negative emotions. They help us stay safe. During our hunter-gatherer days, when there was a bush rustling in the breeze nearby, the people who immediately assumed that it might be something dangerous were much more likely to survive and pass on their genes than the people who sat in silent appreciation of the lovely sound.

This so-called negativity bias worked for our ancestors to keep them safe, but now it continuously brings our focus back to the struggles in our lives and leaves little attention left for noticing the beauty of our surroundings, the extraordinary love we give and receive, and the amazing gifts and "lucky draws" that make up our lives. Not that there aren't boulders in all of our roads—and some of them are quite big and overwhelming—but the road often travels through breathtaking, heart-squeezing, utterly wonderful terrain that our bias causes us to miss altogether.

Appreciation Is Intentional

Like most things, building appreciation for the joyful experiences we have in life takes practice. If we have been focused on trying to control our negative thoughts, feelings, and experiences for a long time, it can be a difficult task to shift our focus to the wonderful things around us (see Microskill 20 for more ways to do this).

TRY THIS: Take right now for instance. As you look around you in this moment, what do you notice? Are you okay? Is anything bad happening right now? What are the things in your surroundings right now that make your heart hurt in a good way? Right now I'm in a toasty coffee shop on a rainy day, next to a beloved notebook and a phone that I could pick up and immediately see pictures of people I love. I'm warm, dry, fed, loved, hydrated, cared about, and generally very, very lucky.

With some practice, noticing these things becomes second nature, and the full range of experiences and emotions becomes more available to us. This is an intentional activity, though. If we do not *intentionally* allow ourselves to notice our positive experiences and emotions, we often miss them. Right before I noticed my cozy surroundings and wonderful things around me, my mind was focused on the distressing number of tasks I need to complete today compared to the amount of time I have to complete them (a favorite line of thought for my mind). But I can notice both the thoughts about my to-do list and the amazing world around me. Opening up to the good things just requires an additional step in my noticing.

Three Good Things

Each day (and right now as you're reading this) write down in your journal three good things that have happened in the day. Researchers have found that doing this every day actually can improve your outlook on things over a long period of time. Just take a few minutes each day to literally take note of the good stuff from the day.

It's likely you'll note all kinds of little things that you didn't previously notice happening throughout your day. My lists often include things like coffee, kind gestures, coffee, running water, coffee—you get the idea— things we normally take for granted.

Just a reminder: the overall goal is to bring mindful awareness to both the good *and* the bad that happens in our day. Bringing awareness to the bad will allow us to back up from it and respond based on our values rather than reacting (see Microskill 8 for tips on backing up and Microskills 12 and 13 for discussions of values). Bringing awareness to the good will allow those experiences to be encoded, appreciated, tied to our values, and lived fully.

Practice Gratitude

When you think about gratitude, what do you think of? Some people think of counting blessings or thank-you cards or appreciation or even wonder and awe at the world around us. It is a common saying that appreciation is the key to a good life. But how? What are the pitfalls? When does it start increasing our tendency to avoid our stuff?

You know what it's really hard to be simultaneously? Grateful and angry. Or grateful and jealous. Or grateful and full of evil, vicious contempt. It's even kind of hard to be grateful and worried or scared. Gratitude has this funny quality that it isn't something that we think about often, but when we do, we can often find a million things to be grateful for.

We all know that it is good to be grateful. You might even know about the large number of studies that have looked at the benefits of gratitude and all of the many things being grateful brings into your life. But knowing that being grateful is important is not usually enough. Even being aware that gratitude can make us feel better or contribute to our life and health in meaningful ways often does not help us feel grateful.

Because consistent gratitude is hard. It takes a tremendous amount of focus to draw our minds from our automatic negative bias toward things we're unhappy with or worried about. And, for many people, almost as soon as that focus is applied, it disappears. Seriously. Consistent gratitude is hard.

Life Is Precious, Until It Isn't

Ever notice that when something really scary happens to somebody, they are often super grateful for their life and loved ones? Maybe you've experienced this too. It's such a powerful feeling, and people often think, *Wow, I'm never going to take any day or any of my wonderful family members for granted ever again.* And they don't, until one day after they have recovered from whatever the crisis was, without meaning to, they lose the sense that life is precious and that they should be grateful for every minute of it.

Benefits of Gratitude

There are many reported benefits of gratitude in the research literature. High levels of gratitude are related to a number of cool things like resiliency, better relationships, lower risk of psychological disorders, and improved health—particularly related to sleep and heart functioning (see Emmons & McCullough, 2003).

Being grateful is thought to bring about a cool life, not the other way around. This means that it's not that people who have charmed lives are more grateful because everything always goes their way, but rather that people who practice gratitude regularly end up having more charmed lives.

Cultivating More Gratitude

Scientists have studied ways to increase the experience and benefits of gratitude. One powerful method to express gratitude is to write a Gratitude Letter—a letter thanking somebody for all they have done for you—and then *read it aloud to the person.* That last part is an important (although sometimes difficult) part of the task. It turns out that reading this kind of letter, thoughtfully written by your own hand, has impacts not only on your overall sense of well-being but also on the relationship.

Another way to increase your experience of gratitude is to keep track of things you are grateful for—in a Gratitude Journal—every day. In research that has studied this, the people who noted what they were grateful for generally rated themselves as having higher levels of well-being after doing this than people who wrote about other kinds of things.

Gratitude versus Gratefulness

Sometimes people find it useful to make a distinction between gratefulness and gratitude. Gratitude is what you feel (and express) when somebody does something nice for you. This is the good feeling you get from thanking somebody for their thoughtfulness (like in the Gratitude Letter exercise).

Gratefulness is a more general experience of being thankful. You can have gratefulness for good health, a soft blanket, or a beautiful sunrise. Unlike gratitude, it doesn't have to be related to another person. Gratefulness is more often what shows up in the Gratitude Journal exercise.

Each of these can be helpful in its own way. Allowing all the many things you are grateful for to be part of your ongoing experience will combat that negativity bias we talked about in Microskill 18—the habit that has been bred into you over thousands of years to pay much more attention to the bad things that happen than the good.

When it comes to counting our blessings, it is feast or famine for most of us—we're either chock full of the love and feeling all the gratitude, or we're stuck in our negative story and unable to see what a person could even have gratitude for. But paying attention to the wonderful things people around you do for you and expressing your gratitude for that enriches your relationships and deepens your connections with people—which is also fabulous.

Daily Gratefulness

One way to bring gratitude and gratefulness into your experience is to systematize your practice of it. It just isn't something we do regularly unless we have made a habit of it. Luckily, making it a systematic practice is easy to do. The Gratitude Journal exercise we described is an easy way to regularly count your blessings. Each night before you go to bed, just write in your journal a few things you are grateful for. That's it. The benefit of doing it right before you go to sleep, according to research, is that it will have the added benefit of improving your sleep quality and reducing insomnia.

If you want to supercharge your gratitude practice while enhancing your relationships, you can add a Daily Thank You intention. Just try to express your thanks—it can be for something small or all the way up to the big stuff—each day, and jot down whom you expressed gratitude to, next to your daily gratefulness in your journal.

Tip Toward the Amazing

Consider what is amazing about your life, like, right now. Who is healthy? What worked out well? How are you lucky? There is so much richness in our relationships, our physical environment, the art and music we experience, and the creative pursuits we follow. If we move through fear to the other side of it, we encounter the richness of life. Wouldn't it be great if we could truly appreciate it?

While there are a million ways that our lives are easier than those of our ancestors, there are also a million ways that our modern life is making it harder to notice the awesome around us. A number of culprits distract us from a rich, full, meaningful life.

Pressure to Look Like We Have a Rich, Full, Amazing Life Distracts Us from Having One

We've all seen them. Social media posts about an amazing experience somebody had (sometimes only to find out later that what looked fun and carefree was actually staged and artificial). Or the "effortless" party somebody put together that required hours of planning and excessive use of Pinterest. Never before have we shared glimpses of lives that could be so purposefully posed and prepared. And this is the standard we are comparing our own lives to. It can lead to thinking our own lives are not so great.

We frequently imagine an ideal life that does not involve all of the unpleasant realness of the lives we are actually in. We compare our real lives to that ideal one and find our real one seems no good in comparison. Meanwhile, this real life is the one we've got, and we're missing all the good stuff by being focused on how non-ideal it is.

We Are Too Distracted to Notice How Amazing Our Life Is

This is the obvious one—we're distracted by technology and forget to lift our heads up and look at the sky or bend over to smell the roses. When was the last time you spent a day without electronics? We're not saying that amazing things can't be found on a screen, but when was the last time you spent a significant amount of time noticing all of the amazing sights and sounds around you? A study recently showed that about half of us spend five or fewer hours in nature each week (Kellert et al., 2017). Five or fewer hours outside in a 168-hour week!

Another thing that distracts us is our ever-running mind. As we've described throughout this book, we humans are primed to look for threats in our environment. Our minds are built for survival, and all this threat checking and survival focusing tends to remove us from all the amazing things that are going on all around us.

We're Addicted to More, Better, Different

A third way that modern life pulls us away from the awesome is more subtle. We can believe that a "good" life contains more "good" feelings and fewer "bad" feelings. This is what compels us to avoid our "negative" feelings, but it is also what compels us to buy a new pair of jeans when we don't need them, and then we find that we wonder why we didn't feel as miraculously happy as the person in the ad was after buying them.

One reason why our new pair of jeans doesn't change our lives has to do with what researchers call "hedonic adaptation" (Frederick & Loewenstein, 1999). The idea is that we experience a spike in happiness when something "good" happens or when we receive something we perceive as fabulous. Quickly, though, we adapt to this new situation as the status quo, and our minds go in search of a new fabulous thing or "good" experience to give us another hit of happiness. This process of seeking a novel "good" thing and then quickly needing a new novel "good" thing when the novelty wears off contributes to dissatisfaction.

The best example of hedonic adaptation I (Jen) have ever seen is from my cat, Kiki. She has a desperate desire to be wherever she is not and is almost immediately dissatisfied when she gets to where she thinks she needs to be. She will stand at the glass door, look outside, and become obsessed (or so it seems) with being on the other side of the door, as though she is sure if she could just get outside she would be happy forever. Almost as soon as we let her out, however, she starts looking through the glass to the inside of the door, just as desperate to be on the other side again. This can go on for hours if a compassionate-enough member of the family is near the door.

The factors that interfere with our ability to experience the amazing are no joke. Luckily, there are things we can do to overcome them.

Awe, Appreciation, and Wonder

One of the key antidotes is engaging in meaningful, intentional behavior that includes a wide degree of variability. A place to easily find meaning and variety is in nature. There are so many things in nature that inspire awe. If you don't believe me, climb to the top of something very tall and watch the sun go up or go down. This happens every day, but we rarely take time out of the story we're living in to actually make contact with it.

Because that is all it is—making contact. You don't get to keep it or put it in your pocket or take it home with you. You just get to make contact with it for the moment you're in, and then move on to the next. In fact, spending as little as fifteen minutes in a natural environment can inspire awe and disrupt the more-better-different cycle (McMahon & Estes, 2015).

There is always a tricky balance between not avoiding your "negative" thoughts and feelings and allowing yourself enough space to be able to appreciate the extraordinary life you're in. Intentionally moving toward things that are personally meaningful or related to your personal values (see Microskills 12 and 13 for more discussion of personal values) can prevent accidentally using appreciation of the amazing things in your life as a way to avoid your stuff.

TEENY TINY PRACTICE
Finding Your Awe, Appreciation, and Wonder

As mentioned above, researchers have found that spending even a short period of time intentionally appreciating nature can have lasting benefits, particularly if we find a way to make a habit of seeking it out. Over the next week, look for opportunities to get outside and intentionally notice and appreciate your surroundings. Shoot for at least fifteen minutes with no agenda, nothing to do—just appreciate the amazingness of nature around you.

Be Gentle with Yourself

There are all sorts of ways in which our minds have evolved to avoid danger. Consider the following: You make a mistake at work, and it was an important one. Immediately, your mind kicks in, saying things like:

You screwed up again. Of course.

You'll never get it right.

You'll never be good enough.

You are a failure.

You don't deserve love.

You are unworthy.

When your critical mind starts in with stuff like that, we suspect that the thing you most feel like doing is curling up in a ball and avoiding the whole situation altogether. And in fact, that's what that critical voice is meant to do—to help you avoid situations that could potentially be dangerous. Could you potentially fail at something? Best not to do it at all. Giving in to that critical voice is another way of avoiding.

But you can't always get it right. Whether it's at work or in your relationships, mistakes happen. It might be unintentional, but there are usually consequences for our mistakes. Even so, sometimes our hardest, most critical judge is our own mind. See if you can slow down and listen to what your mind is telling you about the last time you felt you came up short at something that really mattered to you.

Once, I (Lisa) was speaking to one of my clients—a young university student who struggled with perfectionism. She studied for hours and hours for each test. When she wasn't studying, she was rehearsing facts and answers in her mind. This took up so much of her time, she never got to be with her friends, enjoy family outings, or play. If she didn't get a perfect score, her inner critic set upon her, saying horrible things about her. I asked her if she needed that voice in her head. *Oh, yes,* she said. *Without it, I'd never get good grades or excel in school.* But was she correct about that?

TRY THIS: It's important to observe your own critical voice and see how it works. Notice when and where it tends to show up. You might notice that when you are feeling vulnerable—like after you make an error—it swoops in with a healthy dose of criticism. Or perhaps when you compare yourself to someone else, its negative evaluations kick in. Perhaps it gets louder when you don't feel like you meet your own—or someone else's—standards.

Next, notice what happens once it kicks in. You may find it spins you inward, keeping you spiraled into its negativity. Take some time to observe how you are feeling. Is it really helping? Does it motivate you in the way you had hoped? My guess is probably not.

If you're having a hard time observing how this works in yourself, try this little exercise. Imagine that you are watching a little league baseball game. There's one little kid sitting at the end of the bench in the dugout, some distance from the throng of other kids. Being a good baseball player means the world to him. At home, he practices with his parents every day, and hopes he's gaining skill. On the bench, he's tiny and looks uncertain. When he gets up to bat, he moves slowly, uncertain. The bat is nearly as big as he is. He stands at the plate, waiting for the pitcher, who throws the ball. He swings and misses, the weight of the bat almost toppling him. You hear the coach yell, "You idiot! You'll never be a good baseball player! You suck!"

What's happening inside you right now? Do you feel protective of this youngster? Are you having the thought that the coach is a jerk? Do you think the coach's words will help him build his skill? Consider whether, if you were this kiddo's coach, that's how you would speak to him. If not, then why is it that we speak to ourselves in this way?

Remember, our mind serves as our threat detector. When it thinks we are out of the lane, it does everything it knows how to help us get back on track. This "help" may include really negative evaluations of our work, our intentions, ourselves. It's almost like it needs to say the very meanest things it can to make sure that we never make another mistake, never take another risk, never try something new or different or challenging, ever again. Minds can be so ... *punishing*. Think about it: is there anyone tougher on you than your own mind? It can be easier to be kinder to others than yourself. It can be really difficult to forgive yourself for any failings you perceive. You might think *I don't deserve kindness* or *Ugh, that's too touchy feely*.

Kindness, Not Criticism

It may be that when this inner critic shows up, it feels automatic, like something that just happens, rather than something we choose to do. Maybe, and maybe not. What if it were possible to choose *a different way* to speak to ourselves? What if it's possible to be kind to yourself? Even forgiving.

Noticing our inner critic and becoming aware of how it speaks to us opens the possibility to choose to speak to ourselves another way. Research on how to shape successful behavior says it's important to focus on the *effort* and not the *outcome* of our actions. (Dweck, 2006). Our minds, however, are not so good at that. They tend to go right for whatever our perceived personality faults or shortcomings might be. For example, you might think of yourself as smart or not smart; thoughtful or thoughtless; wise or witless. Instead, think about praising the effort you have put in, rather than the result. Also, you might try getting comfortable with the word "yet." For example, instead of *I can't do that*, you might say to yourself *I can't do that … yet.*

1.   The next time you notice your inner critic kicking in, take a moment to *pause*. Notice that voice, notice what it is saying, and see if you can step back from it.

2.   Ask yourself—*what would a kind coach say to a little, uncertain kid, who has tried really hard to do something that means the world to him or her?*

3.   Practice speaking to yourself in *that* spirit. Hold yourself kindly. Praise your effort. Finish your sentences with the word "yet."

Spread Lovingkindness
to Others

Seems like so much of what we are hearing in the news these days is bad. People are in their opposing political camps; our planet is struggling under the weight of all us humans and our consumption; winning sometimes feels more important than being together. Maybe it is, we don't know (see Microskill 9 to explore the power of not knowing).

Sometimes it's hard to be nice —to ourselves, to the people in our lives who we care about, and especially to those with whom we disagree or who have wronged us or hurt us in some way. It's so much easier to just write people off, isn't it? We can "agree to disagree," but does anyone really feel like that is satisfying? Writing each other off is another form of avoidance. It can feel like an easier way out of a conflict or disappointment or hurt. But is it, really?

TRY THIS: Take a few moments to call to mind an unsettled issue with someone in your life. Perhaps you had an argument. Perhaps you felt treated unfairly, or you couldn't see eye to eye. Slow yourself down—is this resting easy with you? Can you tell yourself to just get over it, and, well, actually do that?

Or does it feel more like a heavy stone you carry around in your chest that gets heavier when you think of that person or when a similar situation arises? How long have you been carrying that weight around? Consider what it would be like to put it down—to *really* put it down.

Just like writing people off or, "canceling them out," holding on to hurt can also be a form of avoidance, one in which we try to protect ourselves from hurt by gathering ourselves up in a blanket of anger and but-I-was-rightness (see Microskill 11). But what does this get us? We think it gets us a pocket full of heavy stones.

My (Lisa's) dad is a pretty tough guy. When I was a teenager, he taught me to ski. I was so excited—I'd had a few lessons when I was younger, but I'd never really done much more than the bunny hill. His way of teaching was to take me to the top of a mountain, bring me to the top of a black diamond (really hard) run, and say, "See you at the bottom!" I was terrified and frustrated, and I fell down over and over and over again, but eventually, long after he had made it to the bottom, I slid-skidded-tumbled down to where he stood at the end of the run. I held back my tears. I wanted him to think I was tough. Inside, though, I was so mad and sad that he left me all alone to struggle. It wasn't fair. I needed help, and I didn't get it. And I couldn't ask for it, either.

I'm sure all of us have stories about how we learned to "suck it up" and power through hard stuff. That might be our way, instead of letting ourselves feel vulnerable. But what if there's something important for us to learn in the stuff that hurts?

My dad loves me. Misguided as his teaching methods might have been, they were all about helping me get along in the world in the best way he knew how. Maybe that was how his father taught him to be tough. And the only way for me to touch that truth was to open up to the sadness and hurt inside—that heavy stone—like a geode that you can crack open to see the beauty within.

Despite all the difficulty relationships bring to our lives, we are inherently connected, social animals. Being intimately connected to other humans is not simply a positive experience in our lives—it is how we are wired. Isolation and alienation are among the most difficult experiences we encounter. What we often forget when we are struggling with other people is how much the person we are struggling with is also just a human being, seeking refuge from isolation and alienation. They also have conflicts and struggles, they also have people they want to write off in order to protect themselves and hurts they've held on to too long. In the end, we're all in this together, even the people we have the hardest time with.

Lovingkindness Meditation

Just like most of the things we have covered in this book, opening your heart when it is contracted with hurt and pain takes a lot of practice. Luckily, we have lots of opportunities to practice this one—pretty much everybody in our lives will let us down. Usually multiple times.

One way to actively keep your heart open when someone hurts you—to put down the heavy stones that you carry—is to practice sending lovingkindness. It's like sending love instead of becoming about the hurt.

1. Sit in a way you can sit comfortably and take a few deep breaths to settle in to your body. When your mind is settled into the present, bring to mind somebody who is easy to feel love for. It can be a pet, a family member, a teacher, or even a character. You don't have to know them in person—just anybody who brings a feeling of love to your heart.

2. See if you can feel the sensations of love somewhere in your body—maybe in your chest or in a smile on your lips. It's okay if you don't feel any sensations.

3. Slowly and with intention, repeat the following phrases in your head, sending them directly to the person (or critter): "May you be safe. May you be healthy. May you be

peaceful. May you have ease." Do this for a few cycles to start, working up to a few minutes.

4. Send the sensations, feelings, or phrases to yourself: "May I be safe. May I be healthy. May I be peaceful. May I have ease." Again, do this for a few cycles to start, working up to a few minutes.

5. Send these sensations, feelings of lovingkindness, and phrases to all people everywhere: "May all beings be safe. May all beings be healthy. May all beings be peaceful. May all beings have ease." Again, do this for a few cycles to start, working up to a few minutes.

6. Finally, send the sensations, feelings of lovingkindness, and phrases to someone you are struggling with: "May you be safe. May you be healthy. May you be peaceful. May you have ease." Again, do this for a few cycles to start, working up to a few minutes.

You can practice this as often as you like. Note that in order to do this last one, you need to be willing to stop avoiding the hurt feelings you are carrying by holding your heavy stone. This can be tough to do, but repeated practice of the Lovingkindness Meditation can help loosen its hold.

PART SIX

Get Through Avoidance Urges and Get Going: On the Spot Strategies

We've been guiding you to develop the following set of skills: to flexibly notice what you're experiencing—just as it is—while bringing gentle awareness to it and considering what is most meaningful to you in the situation so you can move toward those stated values with intentional actions.

Now, no matter how well you learn these skills, it is unlikely that you will be able to do this all the time. There will always be times that avoidance pops up. The goal cannot be that you have to do this perfectly—it just isn't possible. So this last section provides go-to strategies for when you need them because avoiding your experience feels so compelling.

Microskill 23 describes some key ways that your mind can trap you—with rulemaking, predicting, catastrophizing, mindreading, and personalizing—and provides ways to notice and break free from those influences. Microskill 24 offers nine ways to disentangle from your mind when you're really stuck in a loop or struggling with a feeling you want to avoid. Finally, Microskill 25 offers ten ways to become more willing with the pain you experience, so you can move toward what you care about even if the pain is there.

Five Thinking Traps to Notice and Spring Free From

Navigating a complicated world requires that we take mental shortcuts. There's no way to process all the information that comes our way without doing so. Mental shortcuts allow us to sort things into categories, make predictions about the future, estimate the likelihood of events, create personal rules for living, and on and on. Other animals don't do these things. We have the capacity for language; they don't. (I know your parakeet might say everything you say, but that's not the same thing.)

These shortcuts, however necessary, can evolve into traps that drive fear, fuel avoidance, and prevent you from doing what matters. For example, the capacity to predict can snowball into excessive worry about the future. And guidelines for how to live (e.g., be nice to others) can calcify into rigid rules that leave no wiggle room (e.g., don't speak your mind because you might hurt someone's feelings). These "thinking traps" can lure you into avoiding what really counts in your life.

Here are some thinking traps. If you are aware of them, you might be able to sidestep them before they catch you—or spring free of them when you discover you're captured.

Thinking Trap 1: Excessive Evaluations

Our minds are built to judge. Many of our thoughts are some version of "this is good" or "this is bad." This was quite useful to our caveman ancestors trying to make it through the day without starving. "This berry? Poison—bad. This berry? Sweet and delicious—good."

But what about now? Do we need all the judgments we make? Surely, we need some of them. We need to evaluate what's the best house to rent or buy, what's the best diet for our health, and what to binge-watch on a Saturday night.

A lot of our evaluations just increase our suffering. For example, we tend to call some thoughts and feelings "good" and some "bad." But we still have the good ones and the bad ones, whether we like them or not. And then we get the discomfort of painful thoughts and feelings plus the misery of judging ourselves for having them, which is outside of our control. Awesome, huh? And then we stay away from important things that evoke that discomfort, like really looking at our finances, visiting a sick friend, or ending a bad relationship.

It's not just the internal stuff we judge. It's everything. Notice how evaluations might get in the way of engaging in your relationships (e.g., *My partner is a bad listener*), fun things like socializing and sex (*This is not as good as I imagined it would be*), and appreciating small pleasures (*This $5 coffee would be better if it wasn't so bitter*).

Thinking Trap 2: Rigid Rules

Watch out for imposing rigid rules on yourself, the world, and the people around you. These kinds of rules usually include words like "should," "must," or "have to." There's nothing wrong with standards, but these are standards that are inflexible and self-defeating: "If it doesn't make me happy, I shouldn't do it," "People have to be kind to others at all times," "This shouldn't be this hard!" All of this leads to unnecessary avoidance. But what if we lived in the world as it is? What would that make possible?

That rule—*things shouldn't be this hard*—is one that plagues me (Matt). If I'm working on a project like this book, and I get bogged down, struggling to find a direction, I can get pretty angry. "This should be fun—I get to write a book on something I love with people I adore. What's wrong with me?" But if I pay attention to what writing is actually like, based on years of experience, I know that it's got ups and downs. Sometimes you're flying high about the brilliant way you just expressed an idea; sometimes everything you write looks awful. That's just the way it is. When I check in with other writers, they confirm my experience. So why am I expecting the world to be different? Sigh.

Thinking Trap 3: Overestimating the Likelihood of Bad Outcomes

Humans are horrible at prediction. Have you ever watched sports commentators, political pundits, or economic forecasters predicting the likelihood of some important event? Their success rate is about as good as a coin toss. Yet, even though "expert" prediction often fails, the average human can be pretty convinced they know how likely it is that something will happen.

This is called probability overestimation. And it can be especially problematic when we overestimate the probability of something bad happening. It becomes a great reason for avoidance or simply worrying your way through life. This thinking trap also shows up in my writing. Let's say I decide I'm going to write between four and six in the afternoon on a Sunday. I can spend the entire day beforehand, when I could be fully enjoying my coffee and newspaper or taking a walk with my wife, worrying about the likelihood that I won't get enough done or feel sufficiently productive. Meanwhile, I'm not present to what I'm doing. And how accurate am I? Writing often goes much better than I anticipated.

Thinking Trap 4: Catastrophizing

Catastrophizing means assuming that when something negative happens, it's not just going to suck, it's going to be horrible. It's making a mountain out of a molehill. Catastrophizing is best friends with probability overestimation. They usually hang out together, drinking beers, cracking jokes, and making people miserable. Catastrophizing often involves an assumption that things will be so horrible that you can't stand it or deal with it. But check in with yourself: how often does that actually happen? You're probably more resilient than you think. I know I am: when writing doesn't go "well," I usually handle it just fine. The world doesn't end. In fact, I've begun to see the difficult moments as part of the creative process: moments of feeling stuck often lead to new, more exciting directions.

Thinking Trap 5: Mind-Reading

Somehow, we assume we know what's going on in the minds of others. This can be useful. As children grow, they eventually begin to be able to take the perspective of others and imagine the motivations and feelings of the people around them. This is really good for social development. Unfortunately, we can get very attached to our assumptions. And when we do, we ignore other possibilities— ones that have nothing to do with what we think.

In my writing process, what's often at the back of my mind are the imagined judgments of other people: coauthors, editors, other people in the field, readers. None of those people are in the room when I'm writing—it's just me and my mind. I don't know what other people think, especially what they are going to think in the future. And it's not worth the time spending so much energy going around in circles about it.

This list of thinking traps is not exhaustive. You can probably think of a few I haven't listed, like black-and-white thinking, over-focusing on what's not fair, and dwelling on the past. And the patterns we described in earlier chapters, like trying to be right and focusing on the truth of thoughts rather than their workability, can also be called thinking traps. When we fall into them, we are more likely to give credence to our fears and stay away from what matters.

TEENY TINY PRACTICE
Labeling Your Thinking Traps

When you're feeling stuck or unwilling to do something that matters in your life, like go to the gym, listen to your kid as she describes her day, or work collaboratively with a colleague, check in with your mind. Are you falling into a thinking trap? Are you falling into multiple thinking traps? Label the thinking traps without trying to change them and see what opens things up for you. Ask yourself: if I wasn't listening to these thoughts, what would I be doing?

Nine Ways to Disentangle from Your Mind

Some thoughts are bullies. They bump into us when they walk by, knocking us off our feet. They push us around and egg us on to do things that we regret. They show up when we are most vulnerable and suck the life out of everything we do. Maybe your bullies say, "You're a bad person," "You'll never amount to anything," or "You'll never be good enough." Maybe they say, "You can't trust anyone," or "No one will ever love me." Or maybe they are less dramatic but just as insidious: "You can put this off till later," or "You can't handle your emotions." Whatever they say, when we let them be in charge, we tend to do the things that get in the way of living fully. We don't engage our work meaningfully, we don't build deep connections with people, and we don't take pleasure in the beautiful things life offers us.

When you stop avoiding, face your fears, and do what matters, your bullies will get mad, and when they get mad, they get loud. They will scream, yell, and do everything in their power to trip you up. They don't like change. And they don't want to see you succeed.

Here are nine strategies you can use to respond to them in new and different ways. Notice that there's no arguing, fighting, or pushing your bullies away in any of these strategies. They are not about blocking your thoughts out. That just makes them more powerful. It's about learning to coexist with them without so many bumps and bruises.

1. Add Some Linguistic Distance

When you notice a bullying thought, say to yourself, silently, *I'm having the thought …* or *I notice I'm thinking …* or *My brain is telling me …* and then say the thought. So you might say, *I notice I'm thinking that no matter how hard I try, I will never be a good enough father.* Say it with a tone of detachment and non-judgment. You're just noticing, and you are noticing that you are noticing (see Microskill 2 for more about noticing the noticer).

2. Trace the History of Your Thought

Ask yourself how long this thought has been showing up, even if it hasn't shown up in exactly this form. You might notice that a thought like *I'm not as smart as that person* is an old, habitual evaluation that tends to arise whenever you encounter someone who seems pretty sharp. And maybe that thought started showing up in high school, elementary school, or earlier. If the thought has a long history, it's likely more of a habit than an accurate depiction of the world around you.

3. Name the Story

If the thought is one that shows up over and over again, give it a name: *There it is again, the "I'm Not Good Enough" story my mind keeps telling.* Or I *notice I'm getting pulled in by the "Relationships Just Aren't Worth It" story.* Naming it separates it from you, so that it becomes one part of you, not the sum of you.

4. Mindfully Watch Your Thoughts

In your mind's eye, imagine stepping back from your thoughts and watching them as they go by. Notice that your mind continuously pumps out thoughts throughout the day. You might consider imagining that you are sitting by a stream and that each thought could be placed on a leaf floating by. Appreciate how amazing—and how relentless—the word machine is.

5. Say It Fast, Say It Slow

Mix up the way you say and hear the thought by repeating it over and over at high speed—go for at least thirty seconds. Or you could say it to yourself as slowly as possible, perhaps in a deep voice, like an audio track that has been slowed to half speed. When you change up the way you say a thought, you begin to notice it for what it is—a collection of words and sounds—instead of a "truth."

6. Examine the Usefulness of Your Thought

This is the workability meter from Microskill 10, but it belongs in this list. Ask yourself, *Is this thought useful to me right now?* If it's an especially troublesome thought, the answer will probably be no. But imagine other situations in which it might be useful. Context and tone matter. *I need to get my sh*t together*, said with a tone of harsh judgment when you are doing your best but feeling vulnerable, might not be a useful thought. When said with compassion and gentle encouragement, in a way that opens up the possibility for actual change in your behavior, its effect might be different.

7. Make Your Thought an Object

Embody your thought in an object, like a rock, a paperweight, or stress ball. Or write it on a 3 x 5 card. Get playful with the object: carry it around with you like an invited guest, set it on your desk next to you while you work, or use it to play catch with your partner. Notice that you can hold it in front of you, observing from a small distance. Notice that you are bigger than the object. Notice that you are in charge of your life, not the object—even if it's close by. Just like your thought.

8. Notice Past, Future, and Present

Set a timer for a short period of time—two or three minutes. Whenever you notice a stray thought, mentally label it as "past," "future," or "present." You will likely notice most of your thoughts are about the past and future. Humans are prone to dwelling on what's already occurred and worrying about what hasn't happened yet. It may be helpful to do this on paper, writing your thoughts down as they occur, and labeling them as you go.

9. Make a Song

Try singing your thoughts. Make up your own tune, or sing them to the tune of something familiar, like "The Itsy-Bitsy Spider" or "Bootylicious." Keep singing till you notice the absurdity. Just like saying your thoughts fast or slow, you begin to develop a new relationship with the thoughts, connecting to their essential word-ness, not what they are trying to say.

The goal of these exercises is to get some distance from your thoughts, drain them of their power, and open up a space to do something different. For example, if a thought like *This is too hard* or *I'm going to be judged* keeps you from doing something important, like looking for that new job or being honest with your partner, these techniques can make those thoughts lighter, less powerful, less likely to push you around.

Not every technique will work for you. You might have to try a couple of them out. As you get good at using them, you'll likely develop new ones of your own.

Practicing Defusion

The strategy embedded in these techniques is called "defusion." Defusion means noticing the process of thinking and undermining the power of thoughts to unnecessarily guide your actions. When a thought is the primary lens through which you see the world, you are said to be "fused," as in stuck to it or "one" with it. If you are *defused*, you are separate, distant, and more free.

Practice a few of these defusion techniques with a thought that usually gets sticky for you. Identify which techniques might be most effective when you really need them—when you're feeling overwhelmed or just plain sucky, and you're tempted to avoid what really matters. Then, the next time one of those thoughts shows up and supercharges your tendency to avoid, try bringing out a few of these techniques to get some distance.

Ten Strategies for Showing Up with Willingness

When you find yourself avoiding something important, remember that avoidance is not a problem of laziness. "Laziness" is just about the least useful way to explain avoidance. Instead, it's better to think of avoidance as a problem of ineffective control: by avoiding a meaningful but difficult task (e.g., exercising, calling an old friend you've lost touch with), you are likely also trying to avoid the thoughts and feelings that would arise were you to do that task (e.g., boredom, guilt). In effect, you're trying to control those feelings by staying away from situations that evoke them. But it doesn't make them go away for good—in fact, it usually makes them linger.

The alternative is willingness. Willingness (described in Microskill 6) means being open to what shows up as you move toward what's important. Just about every chapter in this book can facilitate willingness, and we've also identified ten teeny tiny practices in this chapter that can be especially useful. Some overlap with other microskills, and all of them can be used to help you stop avoiding and move forward with willingness.

1. Be Mindful of Your Experience

Step back and mindfully watch what's going on inside of you. Do your best not to try to change or control anything. Simply allow what's there to be there. Observe your thoughts and feelings with curiosity, noticing where they begin and end, where they feel most intense, and where they are absent altogether. Watch what your mind wants to add to them, like *What's wrong with me?* or *Why can't I just get over this?* Just observe them come and go.

2. Imagine You Are a Vast Space

As you mindfully watch your experience, imagine that you are not only big enough to hold it (which you are), but that the space inside you is vast and open. There's more than enough room for your thoughts and feelings. You are big enough and sturdy enough to carry them all.

3. Describe Your Experience

Use simple words to narrate the experience to yourself: "I'm noticing that I'm feeling anxious as I'm about to give this presentation." "I notice a heavy sensation in my forehead and chest." "My mind is offering me memories about Mom before she died." "I'm having the urge to do something else besides this task." Do your best to stick to the facts. Try not to add any commentary (e.g., "This always happens!" "I hate this.")

4. Adopt an Open Posture

Adopt an open posture: let your arms rest at your side, bend your elbows, and hold your hands out in front of you with your palms facing up. If you are sitting, allow your arms to rest on your legs. This posture is a physical cue to remind you to stop struggling and open up. Welcome whatever shows up as you move forward.

5. Adopt a Tiny Smile

Relax your face and lift the corners of your mouth ever so slightly. Just like with the open posture above, this is a physical cue reminding you to lean in and let go.

6. Be Intentionally Kind to Yourself

Offer yourself compassionate statements that encourage willingness:

- "Every emotion has a beginning, middle, and end."

- "This doesn't have to go away before I move forward."

- "I can be gentle with myself while I do this."

- "Just because I'm worried, that doesn't mean there's something wrong with me. That's just part of being human."

- "I don't have to make this go away. It will pass on its own."

- "What can I learn from this feeling? What is it trying to tell me?"

Devise your own. Make sure they aren't control statements masquerading as willingness (e.g., "If I can just accept this, it will go away.")

7. Physicalize It

Imagine your thought or feeling is an object. What color is it? What shape is it? Describe its size, texture, and density. Is it moving or still? Draw it on a piece of paper or list its characteristics if that makes it more real.

8. Pick a Metaphor

Use metaphors to make willingness more intuitive. Through language, metaphors borrow the characteristics of one action, usually something physical (watching clouds in the sky), and apply them to another action ("watching" your thoughts). Consider adopting one of these willingness metaphors or devise your own. It helps if you really imagine yourself doing these things. For example, really imagine holding your anxiety as if it's a butterfly. It might help to physicalize it by doing strategy 7 first.

- "Hold it lightly like a butterfly."

- "Wrap your arms around it, like it's a small, furry animal."

- "Welcome it in like an invited guest."

- "Open up and let go."

9. Make an Avatar of Your Thought or Feeling

Pick an object, something small enough to put in your pocket or backpack and carry it around with you throughout the day. Let that object represent the thought or feeling you would rather avoid. Carry it with you like it's your invited guest or your little buddy. You can pick anything: a paperweight, bracelet, or cell phone. Small stuffed animals are especially useful, because if you can embody that feeling in something cute, it's harder to hate on it. It's a practice of welcoming what's there, rather than trying to stay away from it.

10. Act Contrary to Your Action Urge

Notice where your emotion is pulling you and compassionately do the opposite. Remember, every emotion has an action urge (see Microskill 4), but you don't have to follow it.

- If fear is encouraging you to run away, run toward instead.

- If sadness is telling you to withdraw, lean in.

- If anxiety is telling you to speed up, slow down.

- If anger is pushing you to lash out, step back.

- If guilt is telling you to apologize, don't.

To decide whether to use this skill or not, ask yourself if following your action urge, in this situation, is in line with your values. Does it take you toward who and what is important to you? If not, act contrary to it.

TEENY TINY PRACTICES

You can do any of these practices individually, or you can use a combination of them in sequence. You can also combine them with any of the teeny tiny practices described throughout this book. Remember, this is about doing the hard things that count in your life by being open to the discomfort that arises as we do those hard things. We hope that with these skills, your fear will no longer be in charge, and your life will become more meaningful, vital, and vibrant.

Acknowledgments

We would like to thank all the clients who have trusted us to support them through difficult times and who taught us how to make these skills as understandable and useful as possible.

We would like to thank our mentors, collaborators, and fellow travelers in the scientific community, including Robyn Walser, Steven Hayes, Kelly Wilson, Jaqueline Pistorello, Emily Sandoz, Kate Kellum, Akihiko Masuda, Louise Hayes, and the greater Association for Contextual Behavioral Science (ACBS) community.

We'd like to extend our gratitude to people with whom we have collaborated in our professional lives at Cornell's Counseling and Psychological Services; Lyra Health, especially Clare and the coaches; Little Rock VA; UAMS Student Wellness Program; UA Little Rock School of Social Work; Compassion Works for All; McLean OCD Institute for Children and Adolescents, the International OCD Foundation; the New England Center for OCD and Anxiety; San Jose State University; and UCSF Cancer Center San Mateo.

A giant thank you is due to our collaborators at New Harbinger: Elizabeth Hollis Hansen, Catharine Meyers, Jennifer Holder, Jennifer Eastman, Clancy Drake, and Madison Davis.

And most importantly, we want to thank our family and friends, without whose love and support none of this would be possible: Valerie and Jeptha Boone; Bella, Elliot, Stu, Angela, Derek, David, et al.; Toni Jaudon; Peg Cronin; Rory, Josie, and John Coyne; Evelyn Gould; Vanessa Sloat; Jeff Szymanski; Denise Egan Stack; Hope, Jack, and Glenn Callaghan; Sue Evans; and all the Coynes, Whittakers, Greggs, Hutchinsons, Kockenmeisters, Jaudons, and Foleys.

Resources

These are English-language Acceptance and Commitment Therapy (ACT) self-help books that have been researched in randomized clinical trials and shown to help.

Dahl, J., & Lundgren, T. (2006). *Living beyond your pain: Using acceptance and commitment therapy to ease chronic pain.* Oakland, CA: New Harbinger Publications.

Ferreira, N., & Gillanders, D. T. (2015). *Better living with IBS: A step-by-step program to managing your symptoms so you can enjoy life to the full!!* Wollombi, Australia: Exisle Publishing.

Fleming, J. E., & Kocovski, N. L. (2013). *The mindfulness and acceptance workbook for social anxiety and shyness: Using acceptance and commitment therapy to free yourself from fear and reclaim your life.* Oakland, CA: New Harbinger Publications.

Forsyth, J. P., & Eifert, G. H. (2016). *The mindfulness and acceptance workbook for anxiety: A guide to breaking free from anxiety, phobias, and worry using acceptance and commitment therapy* (2nd ed.). Oakland, CA: New Harbinger Publications.

Harris, R. (2008). *The happiness trap: How to stop struggling and start living.* Boston: Shambhala Publications.

Hayes, S. C., & Smith, S. (2005). *Get out of your mind and into your life: The new acceptance and commitment therapy.* Oakland, CA: New Harbinger Publications.

Lillis, J., Dahl, J., & Weineland, S. M. (2014). *The diet trap: Feed your psychological needs and end the weight loss struggle using acceptance and commitment therapy.* Oakland, CA: New Harbinger Publications.

References

Curtis, R. C., & Miller, K. (1986). Believing another likes or dislikes you: Behaviors making the beliefs come true. *Journal of Personality and Social Psychology. 51*(2), 284–290.

Dweck, C. S. (1986). Motivational processes affecting learning. *American Psychologist, 41*, 1040–1048.

Dweck, C. S. (2006). *Mindset: The new psychology of success.* New York: Random House.

Emmons, R. A., & McCullough, M. E. (2003). Counting blessings versus burdens: An experimental investigation of gratitude and subjective well-being in daily life. *Journal of Personality and Social Psychology, 84*(2), 377–389.

Frederick, S., & Loewenstein, G. (1999). Hedonic adaptation. In D. Kahneman, E. Diener, & N. Schwarz (Eds.), *Well-being: The foundations of hedonic psychology.* (pp. 302–329). New York: Russell Sage Foundation.

Kellert, S. R., Case, D. J., Escher, D., Witter, D. J., Mikels-Carrasco, J., & Seng, P. T. (2017). The nature of Americans: Disconnection and recommendations for reconnection. *The Nature of Americans National Report, DJ Case and Associates, Mishawaka, Indiana, USA.*

Killingsworth, M. A., and Gilbert, D. T. (2010). A wandering mind is an unhappy mind. *Science 330*(6006), 932.

Mauss, I. B., Tamir, M., Anderson, C. L., & Savino, N. S. (2011). Can seeking happiness make people unhappy? Paradoxical effects of valuing happiness. *Emotion, 11*(4), 807–815.

McMahan, E. A., & Estes, D. (2015) The effect of contact with natural environments on positive and negative affect: A meta-analysis. *The Journal of Positive Psychology, 10*(6), 507–519.

Nix, G. A., Ryan, R. M., Manly, J. B., & Deci, E. L. (1999). Revitalization through self-regulation: The effects of autonomous and controlled motivation on happiness and vitality. *Journal of Experimental Social Psychology, 35*(3), 266–284.

Nyhan, B., & Reifler, J. (2010). When corrections fail: The persistence of political misperceptions. *Political Behavior, 32*(2), 303–330.

Westen, D., Blagov, P. S., Harenski, K., Kilts, C., & Hamann, S. (2006). Neural bases of motivated reasoning: An fMRI study of emotional constraints on partisan political judgment in the 2004 U.S. presidential election. *Journal of Cognitive Neuroscience,* 18(11), 1947–1958.

Matthew S. Boone, LCSW, is a social worker, writer, and public speaker who specializes in translating mental health concepts for the general public. He is director of programming and outreach for the Student Wellness Program at the University of Arkansas for Medical Sciences, and instructor in the department of psychiatry. He is editor of the book *Mindfulness and Acceptance in Social Work*, and an Association for Contextual Behavioral Science (ACBS) peer-reviewed trainer in acceptance and commitment therapy (ACT).

Jennifer Gregg, PhD, is a full professor in the department of psychology at San Jose State University; and a clinical psychologist at the University of California, San Francisco, where she works with cancer patients and their families. She is an ACBS peer-reviewed ACT trainer, and has been delivering, conducting research studies, and training clinicians in ACT and other mindfulness-based approaches since 1997.

Lisa W. Coyne, PhD, is a practicing clinical psychologist, author, and researcher who has worked with young people, their parents, and adults with anxiety for over twenty years. In 2014, she founded the OCD Institute for Children and Adolescents at McLean Hospital. She is an assistant professor at Harvard Medical School, and directs the New England Center for OCD and Anxiety in Cambridge, MA.

Real change *is* possible

For more than forty-five years, New Harbinger has published proven-effective self-help books and pioneering workbooks to help readers of all ages and backgrounds improve mental health and well-being, and achieve lasting personal growth. In addition, our spirituality books offer profound guidance for deepening awareness and cultivating healing, self-discovery, and fulfillment.

Founded by psychologist Matthew McKay and Patrick Fanning, New Harbinger is proud to be an independent, employee-owned company. Our books reflect our core values of integrity, innovation, commitment, sustainability, compassion, and trust. Written by leaders in the field and recommended by therapists worldwide, New Harbinger books are practical, accessible, and provide real tools for real change.

newharbingerpublications

MORE BOOKS from
NEW HARBINGER PUBLICATIONS

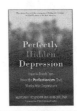